The Life and Times of Gideon

Gideon

The Mighty Man of Valour

MEDITATIONS ON JUDGES 6-8

by
Peter J. Pell, Jr.

Author, "Bible Class Notes on Romans," etc.

ZONDERVAN PUBLISHING HOUSE
GRAND RAPIDS, MICHIGAN

FOREWORD

THE substance of the meditations contained in this volume first appeared in a series of lessons in the Bible Class Edition of "Words of Love." The material has been carefully revised* and for the most part rewritten and is now sent forth in this present form with the hope these chapters may prove valuable as devotional reading. Each chapter has been divided into several parts (usually seven), which, we trust, will also make this volume useful for class study.

The book of Judges, giving the story of Israel's conflict with her national enemies in the land of Canaan, is a rich source of helpful instruction for the people of God today in their struggle against the principalities and powers and the rulers of the darkness of this world, those "spiritual hosts of the wickedness in the heavenly places." That these simple meditations on the life of Gideon may help to arouse the interest of the Lord's people in this section of Scripture, now so little studied, is the sincere desire and prayer of

THE AUTHOR.

---

* The author wishes to acknowledge his indebtedness to Mr. Paul C. Clarke for his assistance in the revision of this work.

CONTENTS

CHAPTER 1

SEVEN YEARS OF DEPRESSION

Judges 6:1-6

"THE Lord is with thee, thou mighty man of valour." Startled by these words, Gideon, the son of Joash, looked up and beheld the angel of the Lord who thus addressed him. In the hollow of an abandoned winepress, stealthily threshing wheat to hide it from the Midianites who had overrun the land, Gideon thought himself unnoticed. But, while no Midianite saw him there, heaven was singularly interested in that lowly man. God saw in him a fit vessel, one whom He would use to deliver His people and defeat the host of Midian. None other would have seen in that quiet, thoughtful, discouraged man God's chosen vessel. But such is God's way. Those by whom He works deliverance are generally insignificant persons. Raised up out of obscurity and endowed with power from on high, they are God's mighty men. Such a one was Gideon.

The background for the story of Gideon is a dark one. The balmy days of Deborah and Barak had been followed by days of gloom and evil. It was a time of misery, desolation and grim warfare. For forty years the land had enjoyed rest, and then the old story was repeated, the story that darkens so many pages of the book of Judges. Seven times over in that book we read, "The children of Israel did evil in the sight of the Lord." And seven times over we read of the Lord delivering them into the hands of their enemies. Just as bright objects are seen to their best advantage against dark backgrounds, so Israel's failure serves to enhance the faithfulness of Israel's God. It is always true that where sin abounds grace doth much more abound. This is seen in God's dealings with Israel. Groaning under circumstances occasioned by their own sin, Israel cried unto Jehovah and He heard them and sent them "saviours." Twelve such "saviours" we read of in the book of Judges. Seven departures, twelve saviours — that is God's way. He is the God of recovery, the God of grace.

For seven years Israel suffered under the hand of the Midianites. "The hand of Midian prevailed against Israel" because Jehovah had delivered His people into their hands. Though the Midianites knew it not, they were the rod in Jehovah's hand to punish His people for their sins. The story of those seven years is summed up in the opening verses of our chapter. Let us consider these verses under six heads, each beginning with the letter "D."

1. Departure (v. 1)

After forty of the brightest and best years in their history, "Israel did evil in the sight of the Lord." We wonder how it was possible for them thus to depart from the living God. The answer is found in Judges 21:25, where we have the Holy Spirit's comment on the times of the Judges: "In those days there was no king in Israel; every man did that which was right in his own eyes." That is man's ideal, but having one's own way is not so pleasant as man supposes it to be. It is accompanied with "destruction and misery," and leads to disaster and ruin. Israel soon discovered this.

2. Discipline (v. 1)

Sin and sorrow can never be divorced one from the other. "Be not deceived; God is not mocked for whatsoever a man soweth that shall he also reap." If we will not enjoy the sunlight of God's face, we shall feel the sting of His rod. Because Israel refused to walk in His ways, they smarted under His discipline, for it was the Lord who delivered Israel into the hand of Midian.

And here is a lesson for us all. The secret of going on well is to keep the eye on Christ. He says, "I will instruct thee and teach thee in the way which thou shalt go; I will guide thee with mine eye." But if like the horse or the mule, we insist on having our own way, the bit and the bridle will guide us. We cannot escape God's disciplinary dealings when we sin against His grace.

3. Defeat (v. 2)

"Midian prevailed against Israel." No enemy could have prevailed against them if they had been faithful to Jehovah, but sin opened the door for the enemy. Who were these Midianites who oppressed Israel? They were descendants of Midian, a son of Abraham (Gen. 25:2), and so were related to Israel; yet they were enemies of God's people. Midian means "strife," and these Midianites were indeed sons of strife, bringing untold misery to the people of God. Forsaking the rule of the God of peace, Israel came under the yoke of the sons of strife.

The history of the Midianites is very suggestive. When first we read of them in the divine record, Joseph is delivered into their hands. They do not hesitate to buy and sell the beloved son of his father for they have no love for Joseph (Gen. 37). Later on they seek to stay the feet of Israel in their progress to the promised land (Num. 22). Failing in this they seek through Balaam to seduce Israel and lure them into unholy alliances (Num. 25:3-18). In Gideon's day they rob Israel of their God-given heritage, leaving them "greatly impoverished."

How much better is the rule of God than that of Midian. Coldness of heart toward Christ, unholy alliances with the world, and barrenness of soul, result when the "sons of strife" rule. James warns us of their power. "Where envying and strife is, there is confusion and every evil work" (James 3:16). "Let the peace of God rule in your hearts" (Col. 3:15).

Let us beware of the inroads of the Midianites into our lives, our homes and our assemblies. Worldliness robs us of the peace of God in our heart, destroys the joy of Christian fellowship and sets aside the assembly testimony to the lordship of Christ.

4. Distress (v. 2)

Mountain sunlight was exchanged for the shadows of the cave, when Israel came under the rule of Midian. Deborah had judged them under a palm tree in the sunny heights of mount Ephraim. Then "Israel came up to her for judgment" (Jud. 4:5), but now in trembling and fear they go creeping into the holes of the earth. God did not desire that His people should be cave-dwellers, and it was a sad comment on their spiritual condition that Israel was brought so low.

Their enemies are to seek "the holes of the rocks, and the caves of the earth for fear of the Lord" in the day when "the loftiness of man shall be bowed down" (Isa. 2:17-19).

5. Devastation (vv. 3-6)

The food supply of His people had always been a matter of special concern to God. In Egypt He had them feast upon the roasted lamb; in the wilderness He fed them with manna from heaven; and when they came into the land of Canaan, all the abundance of its increase was theirs to enjoy. But now the Midianites have cut off Israel's food supply. Israel sowed the seed but Midian reaped the harvest; Israel had neither flocks nor herds, for Midian had taken all. With their marauding bands they overran the land. Thus, in the very place where God had promised them "bread without scarceness," Israel hungered. Through disobedience Immanuel's land had become a wilderness, and the Lord's people, like the prodigal, exchanged the marrow and fatness of the house of God for want and poverty. Midian "left no sustenance for Israel." They had nothing for God, nothing for others and nothing for themselves.

The lesson is apparent. The world affords us no spiritual nourishment. It deprives God's people of their food. If barrenness has invaded the realm of our souls, it is because of our own unfaithfulness. Christ is the food of God's people, "the finest of the wheat" is our portion. When we feed on Him we are satisfied. But it is impossible to enjoy the world and Christ at the same time. When we have Egyptian longings, we loathe the manna.

6. Despair (v. 6)

"And the children of Israel cried unto the Lord."
For seven years God had been waiting to hear that
cry. He allowed the hand of Midian to prevail against
them. He brought them to such extremities that in
their distress and despair they might seek and turn
to Him. That cry would bring deliverance, and become
the key to unlock the floodgates of God's mercy.

Repentance is always the forerunner of revival. God
is waiting today for a cry from His people. There is
much boasting today, and very little weeping. We have
so much of this world's dignity, influence and riches,
that we do not know our true condition. We do not
realize how poor and how wretched and how destitute
we are. If instead of saying, "We are rich and increased with goods and have need of nothing," we
would cry unto the Lord, confessing our personal sins
and the sins of His people as a whole, times of refreshing would come from the presence of the Lord. It
matters not how poor we may be when all God's fulness in Christ is ours to enjoy, nor how feeble when all
power is His. We can be content to be nothing when
He is everything. Let us confess our worldliness, our
waywardness and our wretchedness, and cry unto the
Lord. He will hear that cry, and will work deliverance
for His people.

CHAPTER 2

THE UNKNOWN PROPHET'S MESSAGE

Judges 6:7-10

BEFORE a physician can apply a healing unguent to a festering wound, he must first probe deep into the wound to remove all dead and poisonous matter. In the same manner God deals with the spiritual wounds of His people. When Israel cried to the Lord when oppressed under the hand of Midian, He did not at once send an angel to deliver them. First He sent a man of God to them to expose their sinful condition and show them the reasons for their distress. We see the same order in Hebrews 4:12-14. First the Word of God pierces "even to the dividing asunder of the soul and spirit, discerning the thoughts and intents of the heart"; then the High Priest appears, bringing mercy and grace.

The chief ministry of the prophet was not to foretell coming events but to apply the word of God to the existing condition of God's people and thus to reach their consciences and bring them back to God. Samuel was entrusted with a prophetic message to Eli after the failure of the priesthood, and when David the king had sinned, God sent Nathan the prophet to point out his sin to him. From Samuel to John the Baptist we can trace a noble line of prophets who sought to stem the tide of evil in Israel. Their ministry was never popular, for people then, as now, clung to their sins and were loathe to give them up. When the Lord Jesus revealed the sin in the Samaritan woman's life, she said, "Sir, I perceive that thou art a prophet." The Lord desires to reveal a love that covers the sin, but first He must bring that sin to light. First the conscience is reached, sin in the heart ferreted out, and then the heart is opened to receive of the goodness of God's heart.

We call the man of God who came to Israel "the unknown prophet" because his name is not revealed. Whoever he was, he was a faithful servant of Jehovah and he will receive a faithful servant's reward "in that day." The message he brings to Israel is full of grace. The past dealings of God with Israel are recounted in order that they might remember from whence they had fallen and repent. God was the same; He had been faithful to Israel but Israel had not been faithful to Him. This was the burden of the prophet's message. Against the glorious background of God's faithfulness he points out their disobedience, and their sin is seen to be exceeding because of the grace they had sinned against. Seven bright rays of grace flash from the prophet's message, and then seven short words, a reminder of Israel's sin, cast a deep shadow over all.

1. Salvation (v. 8)

"I brought you up from Egypt." Egypt was the land of tyranny and oppression, of toils and tears, the land whose king had challenged Jehovah when He came to deliver His people. The sore judgments that fell upon Egypt, the blood upon the lintel and side posts of the door, the parting of the waters of the Red Sea combine to tell the story of God's salvation. As a bird protecting her brood beneath her feathers He had hovered over them in Egypt. As a shepherd He had led them through the deep. On eagles' wings He had brought them to Himself. Had they forgotten all this?

The poured out wrath at Calvary, the crimson flood from the riven side of a dying Saviour, the empty tomb and the risen Lord tell a greater story of divine power. "I brought you out." God did it. Have *we* forgotten all this?

2. Liberty (v. 8)

"I . . . brought you forth out of the land of bondage." As slaves in Egypt Israel served with rigor and their lives were made bitter with hard bondage. But the sighing of the prisoner came up before God, and according to the greatness of His power He preserved those who were appointed to die, and came down into the prison house to set them free. He "broke their bands in sunder." No longer did they groan under the lash of the master's whip, nor languish under the oppressor's galling yoke. God had seen the captives toiling at Egypt's brick kilns, His ear had heard their groans, His heart knew their sorrows and His hand was mighty to save.

> "And we have known deliverance, Lord,
>   From bondage worse than theirs by far,
> Sin held us with a stronger cord,
>   Yet by Thy mercy free we are."

3. Deliverance (v. 9)

"I delivered you out of the hand of the Egyptians." What a word that was for Israel when God said, "The

Egyptians whom ye have seen today ye shall see them
again no more forever, the Lord shall fight for you
and ye shall hold your peace" (Exod. 14:13, 14). God
placed them beyond the reach of their former masters
by taking them through the flood as on dry land. The
Red Sea rolled between them and the land of their
bondage; they had left it forever.

How great is God's salvation—the enemy is defeated,
his power is broken and we have complete deliverance
from the world through the resurrection of our Lord
Jesus Christ.

> "The Lord is risen: With Him we also rose,
> And in His grave see vanquished all our foes.
> The Lord is risen: beyond the judgment land,
> In Him, in resurrection-life, we stand."

4. Preservation (v. 9)

"And out of the hand of all that oppressed you."
The God who saved His people also kept them; He
"held their souls in life." They were in His mighty
hand—who could touch them there? Balak discovered
that he could not. Balaam with all his enchantments
could not reverse the blessing of God. Amalek could
not prevail against them. God was for them and who
could be against them.

Of His own sheep Christ could say that no enemy
could touch them. "I give unto them eternal life; and
they shall never perish, neither shall any man pluck
them out of my hand" (John 10:28, 29).

5. Victory (v. 9)

"Drave them out from before you." To the ten spies
the conquest of Canaan seemed an impossibility, but

for Jehovah the Canaanites were no match. Israel did not gain the victory by their might nor by the strength of their arms; God went before them and subdued all their foes. So God gives us the victory through our Lord Jesus Christ. We sing,

> "Grace begun shall end in glory:
> Jesus, He the victory won,
> In His own triumphant story
> Is the record of our own."

6. Possession (v. 9)

"And gave you the land." The Word of God abounds with beautiful descriptions of the land that God gave to Israel. It was "an exceeding good land," "a land which floweth with milk and honey" (Num. 14:7, 8). It was "the pleasant land," "Immanuel's land," where Israel enjoyed every earthly blessing.

Fairer than Canaan's land is the inheritance that is ours. We are blessed with every spiritual blessing in the heavenlies in Christ (Eph. 1:3).

7. Promise (v. 10)

"And I said unto you, I am the Lord your God; fear not the gods of the Amorites, in whose land ye dwell."

The assurance of God's presence with His people was better than all of God's gifts to them. His goodness is but the avenue to the knowledge of Himself. "Happy is that people whose God is the Lord."

Seven bright rays of grace! Every one of them spoke of the kindness and love of God to Israel. God had been faithful in keeping His covenant with His people. Their present condition was surely not due to unfaithfulness on His part. But, alas, the unknown prophet's message could not end here. That little word "but"—many times a blessed word in Scripture, but here a very ugly word—introduces that which casts a dark shadow over the lovely picture of grace: "But ye have not obeyed His voice."

Israel had been delivered from bondage in Egypt, but now they are delivered into the hands of the Midianites. Instead of preservation, victory and possession, they have chastening, defeat and loss. God could not bless iniquity. "If we believe not, yet He abideth faithful, He cannot deny Himself." In every phase of restoration we must learn that there is no failure with God. We suffer because of our own sin and folly. The acknowledgment of this is the beginning of recovery, and to that end the prophet was sent.

CHAPTER 3

"THE LORD IS WITH THEE"

Judges 6:11-16

*W*ITH a flail in his hand, serious thoughts in his mind and an ever-watchful eye, we find Gideon beating out wheat by the winepress of Ophrah. Ordinarily he would be threshing grain in an open space where the wind could sweep away the chaff as the oxen trod out the grain. But now, since the Midianite hordes had "entered into the land to destroy it," grain must be threshed in strictest secrecy to keep it from the hands of the invaders.

Gideon was an overcomer. By diligent care and watchfulness he succeeded in securing wheat for himself and his father's house. And now he had chosen a little secluded hollow among the rocks, where the winepress stood, to thresh the grain and hide it from the Midianites. As Gideon worked he watched, ever fearful of being spied upon. Suddenly he perceived a stranger with a staff in his hand sitting under an oak tree and watching him as he worked. Who was this stranger? Was he a friend or an enemy? Before Gideon could speak, the stranger's voice rang out with an astonishing salutation: "The Lord is with thee, thou mighty man of valour!"

What a greeting to fall on the ears of Gideon! His poverty and weakness were so abject, so manifest, and yet Jehovah Himself appeared to him, addressing him not according to what he was in himself, but according to what God by grace would make him. God saw in Gideon all that He was going to make of him, and when he called him "mighty man of valour," it was because he was going to make him just that. "Little is much when God is in it," is a saying often heard. Gideon was little; God was much. We are going to consider them both, but first let us talk about the "much" and after that the "little."

1. The Divine Visitor (v. 11)

When the glory of the golden days of Joshua had faded away and the declension of Israel foreboded the dark days of apostasy and defeat that lay ahead, an angel of the Lord came up from Gilgal to Bochim. This was a significant action. From their camping grounds at Gilgal Israel had gone from victory to victory. Bochim (the meaning of which is "weepers") was the place where Israel wept because of lost blessings. But God remembered the tears which Israel shed there and He accepted their sacrifices (Jud. 2:1-5). Failure had brought God's people to the valley of Baca, but they found God there and it became a well (Ps. 84:6).

In the days of Deborah blessing reached Israel from the heights of Mount Ephraim. Gideon in the winepress presents a far different picture but a most helpful lesson; we learn that divine power is made perfect in weakness. Let us translate the proper names in verse 11 of our portion and notice how suggestive

they are. "And there came an angel of the Lord and
sat under an oak which was at Ophrah (dust) that
pertaineth unto Joash (the despairing one) the Abiez-
rite (my father is help)."

The oak is the symbol of strength while dust certainly speaks of weakness. If we take our rightful place
in the dust before God we shall find that the oak is
still in Ophrah for God raiseth up the poor out of the
dust . . . to set them among princes" (I Sam. 2:8).
If like Joash we despair of any other help, we know
a Father in whom is our help.

Nor should we miss the lesson of the winepress
where Gideon was sheltered from the enemy and where
he secured his wheat, for this winepress tells us of the
cross of our Lord Jesus Christ. There the grapes of
wrath were pressed into His cup of suffering. There
the blood of the grape — His precious blood — poured
out, secured for us remission from all our sins and
blessings that are eternal.

2. The Divine Revelation (v. 12)

It was at the winepress that the angel of Jehovah
appeared to Gideon. He had appeared to others in days
of old. To Abraham as he sat in the tent door in the
heat of the day, He appeared as a Friend, to com-
mune with him and reveal to him the thing which He
was about to do. And Abraham was called the friend
of God (Gen. 18:1, 17, 33).

To Jacob also, "greatly afraid and distressed" as
he awaited the approach of Esau and his four hundred
men, the Lord appeared. He wrestled with him
until the break of day, crippling his strength but con-
ferring upon Jacob — the planner, the schemer, the

supplanter — a name, which, throughout the coming ages, was to be the symbol of divine power and grace and blessing. "It shall be said of Jacob and Israel, What hath God wrought!" (Gen. 32:7, 24, 28; Num. 23:23).

Moses, as he led the flock to the backside of the desert, beheld the angel of the Lord in the flame of fire out of the midst of the bush. There he received the message that would deliver the children of Israel out of Egypt. One word was enough to combat all the power of Pharaoh. *"I AM* hath sent me unto you" (Exod. 3:2, 10, 14).

Joshua, beholding Him as the Captain of the host of the Lord, fell on his face to the earth and worshiped, glad to be the servant of so glorious a Master, whose will now was supreme. "What saith my Lord unto his servant?" said Joshua as He took the place of subjection (Joshua 5:13-15).

And now Gideon follows in the line of these worthy men, and so, too, may we, for the Lord of Glory still manifests Himself to the believer.

3. The Divine Presence (v. 12)

"Best of all, God is with us." Thus spoke John Wesley in his dying moments to those who stood at his bedside. Though the presence of the Midianites seemed to deny the fact, yet to Gideon was given the assuring word, "The Lord is with thee." Such a word spoken in the days of Israel's glory would have occasioned no surprise, but in the days of her shame, while overrun by her foes, it was another matter. Only faith could receive it and believe it then.

But such words are like a shaft of light amid prevailing darkness. Throughout the centuries the watchword of the militant church has been the parting words of our Risen Saviour, "Lo, I am with you alway, even unto the end of the world" (Matt. 28:20). To this day the feeblest companies of God's people in the most trying circumstances and in the most desperate situations have experienced the blessed fact that where two or three are gathered together in the Name of the Lord Jesus, He is there. His presence is the rallying point, the blessed center, the one great and only necessity for believers.

Moses knew how important was the presence of Jehovah with His people. "If Thy presence go not with me," he pleaded, "carry us not up hence. For wherein shall it be known here that I and Thy people have found grace in Thy sight? Is it not in that Thou goest with us? So shall we be separated, I and Thy people, from all the people that are on the face of the earth" (Exod. 33:15, 16).

4. The Divine Call (v. 12)

In the eyes of the Midianites Gideon was a coward— he had to thresh his wheat in a corner to hide it from them. In the eyes of Israel Gideon was of very little account — his family was poor in Manasseh. Even in his own eyes Gideon was the least and the last. But in the eyes of the Lord he was a "mighty man of valour."

There was no outward sign of might or valor about poor, trembling, hiding Gideon. His strength was not in himself but in the God who "calls those things that be not as though they were" (Rom. 4:17).

In the days of John, the mighty Roman Empire ruled

the world. John had come under the power of it and
was suffering banishment on the lonely island of Patmos. Hidden in the great empire were poor, struggling
little companies of God's people. They were not considered worthy of mention in the annals of the empire,
and if noticed at all it was only to be looked upon with
disdain. But John received a message from heaven
for those feeble churches and they are addressed as
"overcomers." That mighty empire has long since
crumbled to dust, but those saints are victorious with
Christ on high.

To the "little flock" the promise of the kingdom is
given (Luke 12:32). The man whose bodily presence
was weak and his speech contemptible was God's chosen
vessel, mighty through God to the pulling down of
strongholds. For "not he that commendeth himself is
approved but whom the Lord commendeth" (2 Cor.
10:18).

It was God's call that gave character to Gideon.
That made him a mighty man. In later years David
had not a few "mighty men." We read that "they
were all mighty men of valour" (1 Chron. 12:21, 22).
But it was association with David that gave them
that character. No one would have considered them
"mighty" when they fled to the cave of Adullam, es-
caping debt, distress, and disagreeable circumstances.

That is God's way. He takes up a poor sinner, saves
him by His grace, fits him for His presence, and then
enables him to stand fearlessly for Him in the presence
of a hostile world.

5. The Divine Enabling (v. 14)

On one occasion, when the Emperor Napoleon was
reviewing his troops, the rein slipped from his hand

and left him helpless on the back of a spirited horse.
A private soldier, seeing his danger dashed from his
place in the ranks, grasped the trailing rein and handed
it to the Emperor. "Thank you, Captain," said Napoleon, immediately rewarding him with a commission.
Implicit faith in the Emperor's word made the soldier
bold. "Of what regiment, sire?" he asked. And the
Emperor, pleased with the soldier's faith in his word,
replied, "Of my own guard." Whereupon the soldier
did not return to his place in the ranks, but went over
and stood with the officers of the Emperor's guard.

In a similar manner God dealt with Gideon and pro-
ceeded at once to make him what in grace He had
already called him, a "mighty man of valour." "The
Lord looked upon him and said, Go in this thy might."
Thus He revealed Himself not only *to* Gideon, but also
in Gideon, as the God of power.

Jehovah looked upon him, and that look imparted
power. Today, even as then, the "help of God's countenance" is the "health of our countenance" (Ps. 42:5,
11). The shining of God's face is the salvation of His
people (Ps. 80:3), and when He hides His face they
go down in defeat. "There be many that say, Who
will do us any good? Lord, lift Thou up the light of
Thy countenance upon us" (Ps. 4:6).

6. The Divine Commission (v. 14)

From the burning bush, where Moses beheld the
glory of the Lord, he was sent to deliver Israel out
of Egypt. From the winepress, where Gideon beheld
the angel of the Lord, he was sent to deliver Israel
out of the hand of the Midianites. So it was with Saul
on the way to Damascus. God revealed Himself to each

of His servants before they went out to labour for Him.

When the Lord Jesus chose His twelve disciples, it was first that they might be with Him, and then that He might send them forth to preach (Mark 3:14). God desires His servants to be wholly dependent upon Him and not upon man. "Have not I sent thee?" is the answer to every question, the provision for every need and the power for every difficulty. There will be no wavering, no hesitating, no "fatal inertia" in our service when we realize that it is God Himself who has called us to our service.

Without that certainty, however, one may soon become discouraged. Consider, for example, John Mark. He was a young man of excellent character and more than ordinary ability; he came from a godly family and had a background which perhaps included personal contacts with the Lord Jesus during His earthly ministry. Outwardly he gave promise of being a great help to Paul and Barnabas as he traveled with them as their "minister." But he had not received the divine commission and when hardships met him he quickly became discouraged and hurried home (Acts 13:5, 13). Mark profited by this experience, however, and in later years he was a great help to both Paul and Peter.

7. The Divine Assurance (v. 16)

"Have not I sent thee?" "Surely I will be with thee." These two facts are the great essentials to success. Because of them the Lord could add, "And thou shalt smite the Midianites as one man."

When William of Orange undertook the cause of the low countries where the Gospel had progressed mightily in spite of the oppression of the Spanish rulers, he was reminded of the overwhelming power of Spain and the allied nations. "You can never resist the mighty power of the empire alone," they said, and they advised him to wait until he could gain the assistance of some powerful nation. "I am not alone," was his answer, "I have formed a league with the King of kings and the Lord of lords and before Him Spain's power is nothing." Nor was he put to shame. God worked marvelously on behalf of His oppressed people, and Spain discovered, as will every nation that fights God, that "there is no wisdom nor understanding, nor counsel against the Lord. The horse is prepared against the day of battle but safety is of the Lord" (Prov. 21:30, 31).

May we all realize in full measure the truth of these precious words. This divine assurance is all we need, but without it we cannot go on. In any little service for God, I must know that I am doing the very thing to which He has called me, and I must realize His divine presence. "Apart from Me ye can do nothing." "I can do all things through Christ which strengtheneth me."

CHAPTER 4

"MIGHTY MAN OF VALOUR"

Judges 6:11-16

*E*VERY work of art has its beginning in the mind and heart of the artist. The sculptor does not think of the rude, rough stone before him in terms of what it is, but in terms of what he is going to make it. "This stone has possibilities," he says, but we all know that those possibilities can only be realized under the skillful hands of the artist.

In our last chapter we considered the Divine Artist. We saw a little of His wonderful power and wisdom and grace that worked in and through Gideon to make him a "mighty man of valour." "Little is much when God is in it." God was much, Gideon little; but in the little that Gideon was God saw possibilities. Let us now consider some of the things in Gideon which made him a vessel which God could use.

1. Gideon was an overcomer (v. 11)

The increase of the land of Canaan was given by God to His people Israel. "The land shall yield her fruit, and ye shall eat your fill, and dwell therein in safety" (Lev. 25:19). Because Israel sinned God allowed the Midianites to destroy the increase of the earth. But Gideon overcame; he would not surrender

28

his God-given portion. He had wheat though Israel as a whole was robbed of it. Not only for himself and his father's house, but for the Lord as well—"unleavened cakes and an ephah of flour" (v. 19)—Gideon had reserved a portion out of the hands of the Midianites.

"The wheat" speaks of Christ the Food of His people. (See Isa. 28:25, Deut. 32:13, Ps. 147:4.) Satan will do his utmost to rob us of "the wheat" leaving our souls "dried away" and our strength gone and "the meal offering" missing from the table of the Lord.

2. Gideon was unselfish (v. 13)

He could not think of himself apart from all the people of God. He was not like Heber, who severed himself from his family (Jud. 4:11), but like Moses he must be identified with Israel even in this sad condition. He quickly changes the "thee" to "us" as he answers the angel. "If God is with me," he reasons, "He must be with all His people." He can only think of himself as a part of the whole.

Like Elijah who took twelve stones "according to the number of the tribes of the sons of Jacob," he identified himself with his brethren. Like Daniel, he felt the burden of Israel's sin. How important that we, too, should have similar thoughts and a like attitude toward the children of God, our brethren in Christ. The divided condition of the church has in no sense altered the truth that there is one body and that we are members one of another.

3. Gideon had an exercised heart (v. 13)

He was not like Gallio who "cared for none of those things" and whose name to this day is the symbol of stolid indifference. Gideon cared. "Oh, my Lord," he said, "if the Lord be with us, why then is all this be-fallen us?" He had a heart for the people of God. He had pondered the ways of God with Israel, for he was acquainted with their history. He had contrasted their present condition with their past triumphs. As he read the pages of their former glory, he knew the secret was the fact of Jehovah being with them. As he contrasted with that their present sad state, an "if" and a "why" escaped his lips. If God was with Israel, why the defeat?

And is there not an echo reaching us today? Are we not tempted to ask the question, "Can it be possible that God the Holy Spirit is in the Church when at the same time the Church is so worldly and so divided in strife?" We read the pages of her former glory, the record of apostolic days, the triumphs of the gospel and we know the secret—the presence and power of the Spirit of God. We are assured of His continued presence. Then why the present condition? May God exercise our hearts to seek His face!

4. Gideon had the secret of power (v. 14)

"Go in this thy might," was the answer to Gideon's exercise of heart. Had he merely said, "Israel has sinned," or "Satan has driven us to this," there would have been no hope. But he saw God's hand in the cir-cumstances. *"The Lord* hath forsaken us, and deliv-ered us into the hands of the Midianites." And be-cause Gideon recognized God in it all, there was hope. True, the situation was extremely dark, and Gideon himself was utterly helpless; but, while Gideon had no strength, Jehovah had strength for him. That was the secret made known to him—"Go in this thy might."

That was the secret learned by Jacob at the brook Jabbok. In weakness he prevailed. A wounded, broken man, he clung to the One who crippled him and found in Him his power.

Paul, too, learned that secret. "When I am weak, then am I strong," he declared. How could that be? Because the Lord had said to him, "My strength is made perfect in weakness." With such an assurance, Paul could answer, "Most gladly therefore will I rather glory in my infirmities, that the power of Christ may rest upon me" (2 Cor. 12:9, 10).

Have we forgotten that lesson? Is it therefore that the Church is weak before her foes? "Little strength" (Rev. 3:8) would cling to the mighty "I Am."

5. Gideon was a humble man (v. 15)

One who had been listening while a bright girl announced most ambitious aspirations and purposes for her own life, answered gently, "You may be right, dear child, but do not forget that the singing birds build low." The low place is the place of blessing; the lesson of humility is essential in preparation for service for God.

Gideon had learned his nothingness. He said, "My family is poor in Manasseh, and I am the least in my father's house." Such humility is not the way of the world, nor is it the spirit of the age. It is still true that "men will speak well of thee, when thou doest well to thyself," but "God giveth grace to the lowly." Moses learned this lesson in the wilderness at the burning bush, Isaiah learned it in the presence of the glory of Jehovah's throne. Jeremiah confessed, "I am a child," and the great apostle Paul called himself "less than the least of all saints."

How much better it is to humble ourselves before God that He may exalt us in due time, than to boast, as Laodicea did, and then to be humiliated by God's exposure of our true condition (1 Pet. 5:6; Rev. 3:17).

6. Gideon was a dependent man (v. 15)

Gideon had no resources of his own. Surely his threshing instrument was a poor thing to look to as the "wherewith" to go against the host of the Midianites. He needed the "Lord of hosts" for that. "Wherewith shall I save Israel?" was his question. "Surely I will be with thee," was God's answer. Thus, being insufficient in himself, he was cast upon God. But when the eye is off the "wherewith," and centered on the mighty God, all is well. God would deliver Israel by Gideon's hand but in such a way as to secure all the glory unto Himself. To prove God's all-sufficiency we must drop into our own absolute nothingness. Almost without exception we can trace our failures to self-confidence. When we consider ourselves competent and attempt great things, we come to grief. God makes our failures so apparent that they are ridiculous.

David had no sword in his hand to fight Goliath neither had Gideon weapons against Midian. Each went forth unarmed except for being girded about with God's sure word of promise. If God be for us who can be against us? Moses went forth for the conquest of the mighty Egyptian empire with nothing but a shepherd's staff and the Name of the great I AM. Pharaoh was a match for Moses but he was no match for Jehovah. The bodies of the Egyptian hosts on the

other shore of the Red Sea told the story—our God
is greater than all His foes. God never asks us to do
more than just to trust Him. That is all that we need
to do.

7. Gideon was the man God needed (v. 16)

Viewing the sword of a great Crusader, a man was
heard to exclaim, "I marvel that such a common
sword should have performed such wonderful deeds!"
Hearing this, the lion-hearted king bared his arm and
said, "It was not the sword that did those things. It
was the arm of Richard!"

God was looking for a man to lead His people against
the Midianites. What kind of a man did he seek? A
fearless, powerful man, with muscles of iron and nerves
of steel? Nay, "but to this man will I look, even to
him that is poor and of a contrite spirit, and trembleth
at my word" (Isa. 66:2). Such a man was Gideon.

God finds His men in the most unlikely places. He
found Moses in the desert, David among the sheepcotes,
Gideon at the winepress, Elisha behind the plow, Peter
with his nets, Carey at the cobbler's bench, Livingstone
in the cotton mill, Moody in the shoe store. God can
do as much for us as for those who have lived and
served their generation.

Let us take this lesson to heart as we consider the
call of Gideon: if we abide beneath the shadow of the
cross, feed upon the Word of God, have a heart for
the people of God, know that power divine is made
perfect in weakness and humbly wait upon God, we
too shall be used by God for the blessing of His own
and the salvation of precious souls. Let us never forget
that "little is much when God is in it."

CHAPTER 5

GIDEON AND HIS PRESENT

Judges 6:17-24

*T*HE call to divine service had come to Gideon; his training for that service followed. Before his public appearance as Israel's deliverer he had to learn in private as a worshiper, for the strength in which he met the foe was gained in the presence of God. Everyone who is called to the service of the Lord must first have dealings with Him in secret. When our Lord chose His twelve disciples, He called them unto Him first "that they should be with Him," and then "that He might send them forth to preach" (Mark 3:13, 14). Many break down in public service because they have not learned in secret.

Four altars mark the progress of Gideon in the school of God. They are important stages in his education as the servant of the Lord. In Gideon's time altars were forgotten landmarks, for backsliders have little regard for altars. But in former days they had marked the path of the men of faith. Especially was this true of Abraham, the father of the faithful. Altars appeared all along his pathway; fresh revelations and manifestations of God marked his course as the friend of God. The first appearance of God to him made him step out in the pilgrim way. Stranger-like, he wandered here and there, but always where he pitched his tent he built an altar. The tent and the altar were all he possessed in the land of which he was heir. And each altar marked his progress in the knowledge of God. He worshiped in the joy of communion.

We cannot be satisfied with less than that. Our service must be the fruit of our fellowship with God. Jacob was not as apt a scholar in God's school as Abraham was, but he, too, had his altars, and at the end of his checkered life we find him a worshiper leaning upon his staff. The Spirit of God chooses that scene out of his life's story in placing him among the worthy men who trod the path of faith (Heb. 11:21).

The four altars that mark Gideon's path to service speak of acceptance, of worship, of testimony and of separation. Let us consider now the altar that marked the acceptance of Gideon's present and gave him the assurance of his own acceptance with God.

1. Gideon's faith was confirmed (v. 17)

The altar was the divine answer to Gideon's questionings. To the angel he said, "If now I have found grace in thy sight, then shew me a sign that thou talkest with me." So wonderful were the communications he had just received, so great the promise, that he dared not as yet appropriate them. He was like them that dream; it seemed all too wonderful to be true. None other than Jehovah Himself could utter such words as he had heard, but he must receive definite assurance that it is indeed Jehovah, and that he had found grace in His sight. He is like Peter who answered the Lord's "It is I" with "Lord, if it be Thou." Stronger faith might have required no sign as did

Gideon. It might have stepped out upon the bare Word of God. But God honors faith, however weak; He is ready to prove His love to us, and the interest that He has in us. The proof to Gideon that God was for him was seen in the acceptance of the sacrifice; the fire came out of the rock and consumed the flesh and the cakes.

We, too, are brought into close touch with God by the sacrifice. All of our doubts vanish when we behold the acceptance of Calvary's Lamb. Seated now at God's right hand He is the pledge and the proof of the love of God toward us. We have three things in Hebrews 6. First, the word of God—God has said it. Then God confirms His word with His oath—"As I live," says God. God gave Abraham His word and His oath. We have more; we have what Abraham did not have for the confirmation of our faith, we have a Forerunner; One who represents us on the throne, One who has been accepted for us.

> "Now we see in Christ's acceptance
> But the measure of our own;
> He who lay beneath our sentence
> Seated high upon the throne."

2. Gideon's desire was granted (v. 18)

There was something attractive about the visitor Gideon had that day. Therefore it was that he would not let him go. "Depart not hence, I pray thee, until I come unto thee, and bring forth my present, and set it before thee." His heart had been strangely warmed as were the hearts of those who walked to Emmaus, puzzled and sad on the very day that Christ had come forth triumphant from the tomb. Though "their eyes were holden, that they should not know Him," as He talked with them by the way, their hearts were drawn from the cold and narrow recesses of their sorrow into the open sunlight of His love. They wanted to make a feast for Him and He had graciously accepted the invitation into their humble dwelling.

Gideon, centuries before that wonderful event on the Emmaus road, had been similarly drawn to that same divine Person, who appeared to him in angelic form by the winepress of Ophrah. And like them, Gideon invites the Lord to be his guest.

The answer of the angel reveals the condescending grace of a God who will not refuse to dine with one of His creatures. "I will tarry until thou come again." And Gideon did come again. Hastily he made his preparations and returned with his offering to the angel.

The One who accepted Gideon's present and entered the home of the two in Emmaus is still the willing guest of all who will open their hearts to Him. Today He says, "Behold, I stand at the door and knock. If any man hear my voice, and open the door, I will come in to him, and sup with him, and he with me" (Rev. 3:20). What shall our answer be? Oh, let us say with Charles Wesley:

> "Saviour of all, to Thee we bow,
>   And own Thee faithful to Thy word:
> We hear Thy voice, and open now
>   Our hearts to entertain the Lord.
>
> "Come in, come in, Thou heavenly Guest;
>   Delight in what Thyself hast given;
> On Thine own gifts and graces feast,
>   And make the contrite heart a heaven."

3. Gideon had a portion for God (v. 18)

In the day when Israel was starving because of their sin, Gideon was able to spread a feast for the angel of the Lord. He not only had wheat for himself, but he presented an offering, "a kid, unleavened cakes and broth" to the Lord.

Whatever the condition of God's people may be we can always present Christ to God. He is the one gift acceptable in His sight. Of none other has He said, "In thee I am well pleased." Gideon's present was acceptable because it spoke of Christ. From among the goats the kid was taken, its blood was shed, and its life sacrificed to obtain food for the feast. From the threshing floor the finest of the wheat was taken to secure flour for the cakes. The action of the fire secured the broth for the drink offering. Thus Christ was pictured in a threefold way: First as the peace offering meeting our need as sinners and satisfying God's righteous demands; then, as the meal offering, spotless and holy; and finally, as the drink offering, His soul poured out unto death in unutterable sorrow.

In Joel's time, the ministers of the altar were called upon to lie all night in sackcloth because of the withholding of the meal offering and the drink offering from the house of God. The restoration of the meal offering and the drink offering would be the evidence of the blessing of the Lord in response to soul exercise on the part of His people. (See Joel 1:13; 2:12-14.) We have noticed how Gideon was exercised about the Lord's honor and the condition of His people. God repented of the evil; He returned and left behind Him a blessing. The offering was the pledge that joy and gladness would yet return to the house of God.

In writing to the Corinthians, Paul was concerned about the continuance of the offering in its pristine simplicity and sanctity. The blessing of the Lord was linked with the proper observance of the Lord's supper, the breaking of the bread and the drinking of the cup. (See 1 Cor. 10 and 11.)

4. Gideon put all on the altar (v. 20)

According to the word of the angel, Gideon laid the flesh and unleavened cakes on the rock and poured out the broth. Unbelief might say, "What a waste!" but nothing is ever wasted which is devoted to God.

While David was in the cave of Adullam, he longed one day for a drink from the well of Bethlehem. Three of his mighty men, who heard him sigh and express this longing, broke through the host of the Philistines, who at that time were occupying Bethlehem, and drew water from the well. But when they brought it to David he would not drink it. That water was too precious to touch his lips. He called it "the blood of the men that went in jeopardy of their lives," and he "poured it out *unto the Lord.*" (2 Sam. 23:14-17.)

Mary of Bethany spent a small fortune for the alabaster box of ointment which she poured out on the head and feet of Jesus. Shortsighted disciples, led by the treacherous Judas, criticized her sharply for this "waste," but Jesus commended this act of devotion and love. The odor of that precious gift not only filled the house that day in Bethany, but has spread throughout the world, down through the centuries, wherever the gospel has been preached. (Matt. 26:6-13; John 12:1-8.)

Wasted? Gideon had not dreamed of the marvelous

thing the angel would do with his present. When he had laid it on the altar, the fire of God came out of the rock and consumed it. The smoke of it arose as sweet incense to the nostrils of God.

For us the message is clear. "I beseech you therefore, brethren, by the mercies of God, that ye present your bodies a living sacrifice, holy, acceptable unto God, which is your reasonable service" (Rom. 12:1).

5. Gideon beheld God in the offering (vv. 21, 22)

When Gideon had obeyed the angel and placed his offering on the rock, the angel touched it with his staff and "there rose up fire out of the rock, and consumed the flesh and the unleavened cakes." Then, as the smoke of the sacrifice rose, the heavenly visitor also disappeared, thus identifying Himself with the offering. Now Gideon was absolutely sure that an angel of God had visited him. The teaching of this figure is important; it shows Christ as the one offering that has perfect acceptance with God.

When we come to set our baskets of firstfruits down before the altar of the Lord our God (cf. Deut. 26:4), there is a remembrance of Calvary, as here there was a foreshadowing of it. The believer finds rest in knowing that the fire of judgment has done its work, the sacrifice has been accepted, and Christ has gone back to the Father in all the fragrance of that which fully satisfied Him.

6. Gideon saw himself (v. 22)

We have already seen that Gideon was a humble man, with a low estimation of himself (v. 15), but this divine visitation has given him a still deeper insight into his own wretchedness. "Alas, O Lord God!" he cries, "for because I have seen an angel of the Lord face to face."

"Now mine eyes have seen Thee, therefore I abhor myself," was Job's reply to God. "Woe is me!" cried Isaiah when he beheld the glory of the Lord, and Daniel in similar circumstances fell down on his face toward the ground. "Depart from me for I am a sinful man, O Lord," was the prayer of Peter as he fell down at Jesus' feet astonished at the manifest power of the Master of the seas. John on Patmos was overwhelmed by the surpassing brightness and glory of the Man in heaven and fell at His feet as dead.

We must come to the end of self if we would be acceptable servants of God. The sentence of death is passed upon self when we apprehend the presence of God and only thus are we delivered from self, our greatest enemy. We do not really live until we can say, "I am crucified with Christ." Then it is no longer we who live, but Christ lives in us.

7. Gideon received divine comfort (v. 23)

Gideon having come to the place where he had "no confidence in the flesh," was in a position to receive a word of comfort from the heart of God. Three precious truths were brought before him.

First, the fact of *peace*. "Peace be unto thee." The blessed proclamation of peace reached him as he stood trembling at the thought of having been face to face with God. But in view of the altar the presence of God was not death but life and peace. There was nothing between but the sacrificial savor, and on the basis of the accepted sacrifice Gideon passed out of the troubled waters of condemnation into the perfect calm of God's own peace.

The question of sin has been settled once and for ever at the cross. The work of Christ has secured peace, and the word of God assures us of it. The story is told of a man who had lost his son. Someone went to see him, seeking to comfort him. "I hope your son made his peace with God before he died," he said. The old man did not lift his head from his hands, but briefly answered, "None to make." Thinking he did not understand or must be deaf, the visitor repeated his remark more loudly, but the old man still replied, "None to make." Once more the visitor repeated his question, and the old man now said, "Twice I have told you that my son had none to make. The peace he went to heaven with was the peace that Jesus made."

It is very important that we have the peace of God in our own souls before venturing into service for God, for how can we proclaim peace to others when we do not know it ourselves? Therefore the Lord Jesus spoke peace to the assembled disciples before He sent them forth. (John 20:21.)

Second, a word of *assurance*. "Fear not." This put him at ease in the divine presence. Like mist before the sun, doubts and fears fled before that word. How precious are the *fear not's of God!* From Abraham in the plain of Mamre (Gen. 15:1) to John on the isle of Patmos (Rev. 1:17), God's people have heard that assuring word again and again. And why should we fear when we have found favor with God on the ground of the accepted sacrifice? Perfect love casts out fear. "Oh," you say, "that is just what I want, the perfect love that will fit me for the presence of God and remove all fear." You will look in vain to find it in yourself; it is God's love, not ours. And God's love, being perfect, can never rest without our being at home in His presence. He must have us before His face in all the acceptability of His own dear Son. The knowledge of this removes all fear from our hearts.

Third, the word of *life*. "Thou shalt not die." Crossing the sea for the first time, a traveler saw a heavy cloud overhanging the vessel and disclosed his fears to a mariner. "Oh," said the sailor, "you need not fear. That cloud has burst behind us." So it is with the believer and the judgment of God. The storm clouds gathered at the place called Calvary; it was there "the tempest's awful voice was heard." And the storm spent its fury there on the spotless, holy Lamb of God.

CHAPTER 6

FAITH IN ACTIVITY

Judges 6:24-40

*W*E have witnessed the progress of Gideon in the school of God, and now we are to see him enter on his public service. It begins in the hardest of all places, his own family circle and his own home town. Gideon has been alone with God and now he is ready, if need be, to stand alone for God. He has learned important lessons in private and now they must be put into public practice.

Gideon was a man of faith, and he proved it by his works. After his wonderful experience with the angel of Jehovah and the divine assurances he received, important things began to happen. Gideon's faith urged him on to immediate and active service for God. Let us consider the great things which now took place in Ophrah of the Abiezrites.

1. The Lord's Altar was built (v. 24)

Urgent business awaited Gideon's attention, but first he built an altar. He did not put service ahead of worship. His thoughts had been turned from contemplation of self and he now thought of what God was for him in grace. The word of God had revealed

44

that to him. Gideon's faith laid hold of the word of God and found expression in the building of the altar. It was an altar of memorial, denoting the relation in which he now stood to God. It was also the pledge of future blessing and victory.

Worship is always the fruit of having God before the soul. We see this in Abraham, whose altars mark his progress in the knowledge of God. He called the altar where he learned God as the God of resurrection, "Jehovah-jireh" ("The Lord will provide") (Gen. 22: 14). Moses named an altar "Jehovah-nissi" ("The Lord our banner") (Exod. 17:15). Gideon called his altar "Jehovah-shalom" ("The Lord our peace"). It was the word God had spoken to him. "Shalom" in verse 23 is translated "Peace be with thee." Having peace he worshiped the God of peace, the source from which peace flows.

We can join Gideon at his altar for it is not in vain that it is stated, "Unto this day it is yet in Ophrah of the Abiezrites." We have already noted the significance of that place. Thank God, the cross still stands unchanged, and as our souls see the mighty sacrifice we bow in worship and adoration at His feet. It is sad that the altar is neglected in our day. Our restlessness robs us of that blessing. There is far more energy for labor than rest for communion. Service may be in the restless anxiety of the flesh; true worship never is. One cannot really worship without knowing peace, and unless the soul is at rest in the presence of God our service is not acceptable. Amid the religious pretensions of our day, when most professing Christians know so little of true worship because they know so little of true peace with God, may we continue to attend to the altar, the place of access, for "we have an altar" (Heb. 13:10).

2. Baal's altar was destroyed (vv. 25-27)

"And it came to pass the same night that the Lord said unto him, Take thy father's young bullock, even the second bullock of seven years old, and throw down the altar of Baal that thy father hath, and cut down the grove that is by it" (v. 25).

"After every vision comes the testing." Gideon's testing had come. How significant are the words, "that same night." With the experiences of the day still deeply impressed on his mind, Gideon is called to be a witness to the grace he has learned.

"The second bullock," was to be offered. It had been withheld all the while that Midian ruled. Seven years Israel had served Midian. Born the very year that Israel had departed from God, it was a suitable sacrifice, the typical means of atoning for Israel's sins and so removing the penalty. Thus also God would receive His portion, for it was to be offered up as a burnt offering.

"The altar of Baal" was to be thrown down. Gideon had built an altar to Jehovah while an altar to Baal stood in the grove of his father Joash. There it was, the symbol of Israel's shameful slavery. "Baal" means "lord." It is impossible to serve two masters. God will not share His glory with Baal; He will brook no rival. Our God is a jealous God, He demands exclusive right to our affections, our interests, our worship and our service.

Under the cover of darkness Gideon, accompanied by ten of his servants, did as the Lord had commanded him. Knowing that his action might arouse the wrath both of his father's house and of the men of the city, he hesitated doing it by day. To avoid the interruption their opposition would occasion, he did it by night. Stronger faith might have been bolder, but the great thing is he did it.

That night marked the triumph of Jehovah over Baal. His altar cast down, the grove cut down, and the darkness illuminated with the fire of the burnt offering told the story of Baal's defeat.

3. The city was aroused (vv. 28, 29)

Early morning light revealed the fact to the Abi-ezrites that Baal had been challenged. Like the stirring of a hornet's nest, their wrath was aroused against the man of faith who dared thus to disturb their peace. For seven years no one had contested the rule of Baal. Now that one had risen to deliver them from his thral-dom, in their folly they turn against their deliverer. Baal's slavery is more to the liking of the flesh than the service of Jehovah. Baal's would-be defenders might rave, but the ruins upon the hill of the symbols of the former reign of Baal and Astarte, and the smouldering remains of the burnt sacrifice upon the restored altar of the Lord gave mute but unmistakable evidence that the power of Baal was broken, his reign was over. Long the dark cloud of idolatry had settled upon the children of Israel; that morning in Ophrah was the dawn of a new day for them, the pledge of full and complete victory.

The action of faith will always excite the flesh. The world will ever make a determined effort to suppress the revival which is to release the people of God from bondage. Set aside traditions for the simplicity of God's truth, maintain a testimony to the absolute lordship of Christ—nothing will evoke the wrath of carnal professors more.

We may have no Baals of stone or Astartes of wood to destroy today, but there are many other forms of idolatry that call for Gideon bands to wield the axe unsparingly. The wood of the grove Gideon used for the fuel of the sacrifice. What faith gives up in obedience to the will of God is never loss. How often we spare the flesh fearing the loss we may sustain or the opposition we may encounter. May Gideon's example encourage us to put all on the altar for God. Separation must precede consecration, the "second bullock" is to be laid on "the wood of the grove which thou shalt cut down."

The story is told of Mahmoud, who hundreds of years ago conquered a great portion of India. In time he laid siege to the city of Guzurat. Forcing himself into the costliest shrine of the Brahmins, he found before him the figure of a gigantic idol, fifteen feet high. Instantly he orderd it to be destroyed. The Brahmins of the temple prostrated themselves at his feet, and said: "Great Mahmoud, spare our god, for the fortunes of this city depend upon him."

> "Ransom vast of gold they offer,
>   Pearls of price and jewels rare,
> Purchase of their idol's safety,
>   This their dearest will he spare.
> And there wanted not who counseled,
>   That he should his hand withhold,
> Should that single image suffer,
>   And accept the proffered gold."

But Mahmoud, after a moment's pause, said he

would rather be known as the breaker than the seller of idols, and struck the image with his battle-axe. His soldiers followed, and in an instant the idol was broken to pieces. It proved to be hollow, and had been used as a receptacle for thousands of precious gems, which, as the image was shattered, fell at the conqueror's feet.

> "From its shattered side, revealing
>   Pearls and diamonds, showers of gold;
>   More than all that proffered ransom,
>   More than all a hundred fold."

Such an idol is self, who pleads and promises that

> "If we will but let it stand,
>   It has pleasures, gifts and treasures
>   To enrich us at command."

This hateful idol will spend years in intriguing to escape from the hand of God. Not in listening to its pleadings, however, but in delivering the idol over to utter destruction, shall we find our true wealth and pleasure, for jewels of priceless worth await those who have learned the secret of losing their life for Christ's sake that they may find it.

4. A backslider was restored (vv. 30-32)

When the indignant Abiezrites saw the scattered stones of the old altar and the smoke of the sacrifice still curling up from the new one, they began to inquire, "Who hath done this?" As soon as it was known that "Gideon the son of Joash hath done this thing," the men of the city said unto Joash, "Bring out thy son, that he may die; because he hath cast down the

altar of Baal and because he hath cut down the grove
that was by it."

The reply of Joash was a surprise to all. He had
been the leader of the Baal-worshipers, but now he said,
"Will ye plead for Baal? . . . If he be a god, let him
plead for himself . . ." This was a convincing argu-
ment. If Baal was unable to defend himself, of what
profit was he to his followers?

Surely a great change had taken place in Joash. No
doubt his son's courageous act had convinced him of
Baal's worthlessness. He turned to Jehovah because
he could no longer have any confidence in Baal. His
faith was but a faint flicker as compared with that of
Gideon who had destroyed Baal because he knew and
trusted God. Nevertheless it must have been a great
encouragement to Gideon to see this change in his
father. Gideon now stood vindicated before the men
of the city. He received a new name, which distin-
guished him as an idol challenger, Jerubbaal ("Let
Baal contend").

5. The enemy was stirred up (vv. 33-35)

News of the exciting events at Abiezer spread rapidly
and soon reached the ears of the enemy. The Midianites,
together with the Amalekites and other nomadic tribes,
assembled together, a great multitude, in the valley
of Jezreel. The activity of faith always arouses the
opposition of Satan. He will not stand by complacently
and allow his authority to be challenged.

When Moses smote the rock in Horeb and Israel
drank from the refreshing stream that issued forth,
"then came Amelek and fought with Israel in Rephi-
dim" (Exod. 17:8). When a man of faith challenged

the power of Baal, *"then* all the Midianites gathered together and went over and pitched in the valley of Jezreel."

The place was very significant for those who had the discernment of faith. Jezreel means "the seed of God" or "God will sow." For seven years Israel had sowed and the Midianites had reaped. What God sows no enemy will reap. God will reap the full harvest of His sowing in the coming day of Jezreel that indeed will be great, when the sons of the living God inherit their God-given portion and no enemy will ever again overrun the land. (See Hos. 1:10, 11.)

6. Resistance was organized (vv. 34, 35)

"When the enemy shall come in like a flood, the Spirit of the Lord shall lift up a standard against him" (Isa. 59:19). This truth was demonstrated in Israel in that day. The enemy hosts marshalled in the valley of Jezreel might well enough have completely discouraged the men of Israel, had Jehovah not given them a leader, though they were sick enough of the oppression of Midian. Gideon, the idol-smasher, was the standard that God raised up that day, and to him the men of Israel gathered.

We have seen that Gideon began his service in the hardest of all places, his own father's house and his own home town. But his faithfulness at home had good results. First his own father was led back to the Lord, and then the Abiezrites, his fellow-townsmen, rallied to him. After that the men of Manasseh, his own tribe, answered his call, and finally the tribes of Asher, Zebulun and Naphtali came up to meet him.

When Jesus had healed the demoniac of Gadara, He

sent him home to his friends to tell how great things the Lord had done for him. After that we read that he "began to publish in Decapolis how great things Jesus had done for him: and all men did marvel" (Mark 5:19, 20). The same order for testimony may be seen in Acts 1:8—first Jerusalem, then Judea, then Samaria, and finally the uttermost parts of the earth.

We have seen Gideon as a *worshiper* (v. 24) and a *worker* (v. 26); now we see him as a *warrior*. "The Spirit of the Lord came upon Gideon, and he blew a trumpet . . ." Let us pause here to notice some of the marks of a Spirit-controlled man.

The Spirit-controlled man is fearless (v. 34). Naturally, Gideon was timid and retiring, but the enabling of the Holy Spirit made him bold as a young lion. His answer to the gathering of the enemy hosts was to take the trumpet and to blow it. Thus he openly declared war against the Midianites and summoned Israel to action. Gideon would have hesitated had he considered himself and the circumstances. Emboldened by faith he acted in the power of the Spirit. He knew the One who giveth power to the faint and therefore he could press on in a seemingly impossible task. Our God delights in doing the impossible, and faith can trust Him to do it. When fear grips the soul, spiritual paralysis results. When clothed with the Spirit's power the greatest difficulty becomes the greatest opportunity for the demonstration of divine power.

The Spirit-controlled man *has influence* (v. 34). Gideon attracted most unlikely persons by his boldness. "Abiezer let itself be summoned after him" (literal translation). Shortly before they had risen against him to kill him. Now they recognize in him their God-given leader. They could not resist the drawing power of Gideon's courageous actions. Influenced by the Spirit of God he influences others. That word was true of him, "Draw *me, we* will run after thee."

The Spirit-controlled man *desires unity and fellowship* (v. 35). God's promise to Gideon had been personal—"*Thou* shalt smite the Midianites as one man" (v. 16). But like Asher he desired to be "acceptable unto his brethren" (Deut. 33:24). Gideon's first act of power was to win the confidence of his brethren. He sent messengers throughout all Manasseh; who also was gathered after him. He knew, and the enemy knew, that the strength of Israel was in their gathering together. When God's people are in touch with the Lord and in fellowship one with the other, they are "fair as the moon, clear as the sun, and terrible as an army with banners" (Song 6:10). Satan does his utmost to sow discord and dissension in the midst of the people of God. It is his crowning work to disrupt the harmony of the church and render her impotent in the face of his assaults and the opposition of the world. "Divide and conquer," is the motto and method of our enemies. "That they all may be one," is the longing of the heart of our blessed Master.

The Spirit-controlled man is a *dependent* man (v. 36 ff.). Gideon now found himself the leader of a host. The response of Israel to his trumpet blast had been remarkable. But Gideon was not filled with self-confidence. His confidence was in the Lord alone. Therefore he sought a sign to confirm his faith, and God graciously granted his request. The signs God gave him form the last section of this chapter in which we have been considering the momentous events that took place at the opening of Gideon's public ministry.

7. Divine signs were given (vv. 36-40)

The time was ripe, so it seemed, to strike the enemy with a hard blow. But Gideon was not satisfied; he wanted further assurances that God was with him. Therefore he asked for a sign to assure him of God's support. God is willing to confirm and strengthen the faith of His own, no matter how weak it may be, but He will not yield to the petulant demands of unbelief. Thus when unbelieving Jews asked for a sign the Lord Jesus answered, "There shall no sign be given you." But when Abraham asked for a sign to confirm the promise made to him of the blessing of the inheritance, God gave him that night vision on the plain of Mamre, of the smoking furnace and the glowing lamp (Gen. 15:8-17). Starting out on the path of faith the word of God must be enough for us. But once on the road God will multiply evidences to confirm the soul of the rightness of the path we have chosen and also to assure us that He will keep us in it. He will meet our weakness and our fears with fresh assurances of His interest in us and His power available to us.

First Gideon asked that the fleece on the threshing floor be wet with the dew and the ground all around it be dry. This sign was granted. When he arose early in the morning he found the fleece so wet that he could wring a bowl full of water from it though the earth all around was dry. Then he asked for another sign. He put out the fleece again and asked that it remain dry while the ground all around be wet. This sign also was given. Thus by two miracles was Gideon assured of the divine favor on his mission.

Important spiritual lessons may be learned from the dew and the fleece.

Dew is a symbol of the blessing of God. It is called "the dew of heaven" (Gen. 27:28, 39). "By His knowledge . . . the clouds drop down the dew" (Prov. 3:20). In Psalm 133:3 we read of the dew of Hermon descending on the mountains of Zion, and "there the Lord commanded the blessing, even life for evermore." The dew falls by night and disappears when the sun arises in its strength, and thus is typical of the refreshment and strengthening which God sends down upon His people during the night of the absence of their Lord. It will not be needed when the day breaks, and the Sun of righteousness arises with healing in His wings. (Num. 11:9; Exod. 16:14; Mal. 4:2.) Moses spoke of it when blessing the tribes of Israel (Deut. 32:2; 33:13, 28). That it is a blessing, a refreshment sent from God, is evident for God says, "I will be as the dew to Israel" (Hos. 14:5). When the dew was withheld it was for punishment or in discipline. (Hag. 1:10; 1 Kings 17:1.)

The *fleece* may well represent Israel as the flock of God. As the fleece is shorn from the sheep, so the sheep of God's pasture had been in the hands of the shearers. But the woolly fleece saturated with the dew of heaven indicates God's willingness to bless His depressed people. The "bowl full of water" wrung out of the fleece suggests Naphtali's blessing, "satisfied with favour and full with the blessing of the Lord" (Deut. 33:23). Therefore when Gideon asked for the dew upon the fleece he was asking for God's blessing upon himself and the poor persecuted people of God.

And God put the blessing just where Gideon asked for
it. What an illustration of the power of prayer. Elijah
prayed and the dew was withheld from the thirsty
land as a sign of God's displeasure with His apostate
people. Gideon prayed and it fell, first on the fleece
only and then upon all the ground. The prayer of faith
commands the dew, withholding and dispensing the
blessing of God. If we ask according to His will, we
receive what we ask for. The dew on the fleece first,
and then on all the ground, may well suggest that first
we must realize the blessing of the Lord in our own
souls before it can reach others.

Israel was once God's depository of blessing, but today she is like the dry fleece. Yet through her fall
blessing has come to the Gentiles (Rom. 11:10, 11).
Some day both the fleece and the ground will be wet
with the dew of heaven, when "the remnant of Jacob
shall be in the midst of many people, as the dew from
the Lord, as the showers upon the grass that tarrieth
not for man, nor waiteth for the sons of men" (Micah
5:7). "Awake and sing, ye that dwell in dust, for thy
dew shall be as the dew of the herb and the earth shall
cast out the dead" (Isa. 26:19).

All Scripture speaks of our Lord Jesus Christ, and
may we not see in these two signs given to Gideon
a foreshadowing of Calvary? Concerning Him David
said, "Out of the morning heaven Thou hast Thy youth-
dew" (Ps. 110:33, Heb.). He was the root springing
"out of a dry ground" when He sojourned here below.
In marked contrast to the barren scene round about
Him, He was the fountain of fulness, for "in Him
was all the fulness pleased to dwell" (Col. 1:19, Darby
Trans.). And yet He "emptied Himself." He who said,

"I will be as the dew to Israel," cried out on the cross, "I thirst." Full of grace and truth, the only way His fulness might come to us was by the way of the cross. Brought into the dust of death, His strength dried up like a potsherd, His tongue cleaving to His jaws, forsaken by His God, He brought us into all the wealth of God's richest blessings. "Of His fulness have we all received and grace upon grace."

CHAPTER 7

GIDEON'S ARMY

Judges 7:1-8

*U*NTIL now, our interest has been centered on Gideon as an individual. We have seen him as a *learner*, receiving instruction from the greatest of all teachers, the Lord Himself; as a *worshiper*, bringing his offering to God; as a *worker*, breaking down Baal's altar and building the altar of Jehovah, and as a *seeker*, praying for and receiving signs of divine blessing on his mission. Now we are to see him as a *leader*, heading an army that enjoyed one of the most marvelous victories in all history.

The story of Gideon's campaign against the Midianites is one of the most interesting and instructive in the Old Testament. Here we have a striking illustration of the truth in the word of the Lord to Zerubbabel, "Not by might, nor by power, but by my spirit, saith the Lord of hosts" (Zech. 4:6). Never did another commander so deplete his forces as Gideon did before going into battle, never were more strange weapons used and never again so singular a stratagem against a foe with such amazing results and so complete a victory.

As we consider the dealings of God with Gideon and his band, we learn what characterizes true collective

58

testimony for God in a time of general failure. Certain features distinguish those who stand for God as His witnesses, men He can trust and men He can use.

1. Confidence in God (vv. 1, 2)

This is the first mark of collective testimony. Throughout the entire word of God we find this truth emphasized, that "no flesh should glory in His presence" (1 Cor. 1:29). Therefore God has chosen the foolish, weak, base and insignificant things of earth to confound the wise and mighty. Thirty-two thousand men were gathered together at the well Harod. Harod means "fear" or "trembling." We may be sure it was suggestive of the feelings of that army as they saw the Midianites in enormous numbers spread out in the valley to the north of them. Many an Israelite must have looked that day at the assembled hosts and said, "We are far too few." The Lord looked and said to Gideon, "The people that are with thee are far too many." God had to prune that army and reduce its numbers so that the victory could in no possible way be attributed to themselves. The Gideon band was not to be marked by great numbers, but by great faith.

The exact number of the enemy host is not given. We only know that they "lay along in the valley like grasshoppers for multitude." Obviously, Gideon's thirty-two thousand was a pitiably small band in comparison. Not only were they out-numbered, but they were no doubt poorly equipped. A motley crowd of poor, half-starved, oppressed hillsmen, without training and without weapons — what match were they for the well-equipped hosts of nomad warriors whose camels, bearing their supplies and equipment, were "without number, as the sand by the sea side for multitude"?

We can well imagine Gideon, as a wise leader, sitting down and counting the cost (Luke 24:31). But one thing we may be sure of — neither Gideon nor any of his men had any intention of making peace with the enemy. Well they knew what the enemy's terms would be, absolute surrender and a return to slavery. They had declared war on Midian and, conscious of their own weakness but confident in God, they meant to see it through. Yet we may suppose that Gideon had hopes of somehow delaying the encounter until his band could be strengthened, and it may be that he was deliberating how his numbers might be increased when that strange word came from the Lord, "The people that are with thee are too many for *Me* . . ."

Christendom craves crowds, but today as always it is a feeble few who truly lay hold on God. Though we cannot boast of numbers, we have the promise that gives infinite capabilities, not alone to three hundred, but even to "two or three" gathered in helpless dependence in His precious Name. Listen to what Christ said, "If two of you shall agree on earth as touching anything that they shall ask, it shall be done for them of my Father which is in heaven." The secret of that power lies in the fact that "where two or three are gathered together in my name, *there am I* in the midst of them" (Matt. 18:19, 20). And again we hear Him say, "Fear not, *little flock*, for it is your Father's good pleasure to give you the kingdom" (Luke 12:32). Sheep are helpless and children are dependent, but such are the heirs of the coming kingdom.

2. Courage in Danger (v. 3)

This is the second mark of God's true witnesses. Confidence and courage always go together. "In God have I put my trust: I will not be afraid what man can do unto me," was the boast of David "when the Philistines took him in Gath" (Ps. 56). Only a true heart makes a strong hand, and therefore it was necessary for Gideon to be sure that every man in his army was dependable.

The first burst of enthusiasm that had followed the trumpet blast in Abiezer had subsided and many of Gideon's followers were secretly repenting the step they had taken as they viewed the opposing army spread out in the valley below them. The Lord therefore instructed Gideon to apply the test commanded by Moses: "What man is there that is fearful and fainthearted? Let him go and return unto his house, *lest his brethren's heart faint as well as his heart*" (Deut. 20:8).

More than two-thirds of the army seized the opportunity. For a while, perhaps, Gideon wondered if any would be left as he saw the multitude departing; but when the faint-hearted were all gone, ten thousand of the original thirty-two thousand remained. To outward appearances, Gideon was weakening his hand by such procedure, but in reality he gained by their departure.

There were cowards in our Lord's day, too. When He set forth the difficulties in the path, the cost of following Him, there was fearfulness and faintheartedness. When nothing but Christ remained and everything else was opposed to Him, many turned back and walked no more with Him. Only a few loyal hearts responded with, "Lord to whom shall we go? 'Thou hast the words of eternal life.'" (John 6:68).

Again, in Paul's day, there were many who turned back, ashamed of the testimony of the Lord, and not willing to be partakers of the afflictions of the gospel. But to faithful Timothy he could write these words, "God hath not given us the spirit of fear but of power, and of love, and of a sound mind" (II Tim. 1:7).

3. Concentration in Service (vv. 4-6)

When all the fearful had departed, one-third of Gideon's army remained. Surveying that group, he could say, "I have a valiant army, though a small one. These men do not fear the enemy, no matter how numerous they are." But the Lord said to him, "The people are yet too many; bring them down unto the water, and I will try them for thee there." The water test was simple but effective. Ten thousand thirsty men were brought down to the water and permitted to drink. Nine thousand seven hundred went down on their knees and quenched their thirst with their faces to the water. Only three hundred scooped up the water with their hands and lapped it with their tongues "as a dog lappeth." These men were alert; their mind was on the battle more than on their own comfort. To them the battle was the important thing, the demands of the flesh secondary.

Gideon was commanded to retain the three hundred and to send the rest "every man unto his place." Nine thousand seven hundred brave men were thus sent home, in God's eyes unfit to participate in the battle. The twenty-two thousand who went home first were glad to go. They were fearful and welcomed the oppor-

tunity to leave. Not so these others. They wanted to
have part in defeating Midian but were adjudged un-
worthy.

If such a test were applied today, how many of us
would remain in Gideon's band? We need to be careful
even about the good things in life, for the good is often
the enemy of the best. Good things try us more than
bad things. We are so liable to settle down in the en-
joyment of them that we become entangled in them.
"No man that warreth entangleth himself with the af-
fairs of this life, that he may please him who hath
chosen him to be a soldier" (II Tim. 2:4). A "hand
to mouth" life may mean hardship for the flesh, but it
will make us good soldiers of Jesus Christ.

4. Controlled by God (v. 7)

Now comes the word that marks that little company
of three hundred as God's own. The Lord said unto
Gideon, "By the three hundred men that lapped will I
save you and deliver the Midianites into thine hand."
They were vessels ready for the Master's use.

God help us not to be like the twenty-two thousand
who were faint-hearted. God help us not to be like the
nine thousand seven hundred who were not whole-
hearted. God help us to be like the noble three hundred,
courageous in the face of overwhelming foes, confident
in God's power to save, concerned only in His service
and controlled by Himself. Power is in numbers in the
thought of man, but better far a handful who know
their God than multitudes who are weak and wavering.
God wants devoted and humble witnesses.

Returning home one evening after a day of visitation, a tired and discouraged preacher sat in gloomy

silence in a river ferry. He was awakened suddenly from his thoughts by an exclamation of the colored boatman:

"I believe dat's de cap'n!"

"Who is the captain?" asked the preacher.

"Don't you know de cap'n? Why, he's de man dat saved me!"

And then he told how once he had fallen from the deck of a boat and was going down to a watery grave with his feet tangled helplessly in ropes. No man aboard seemed willing to risk his own life to save that of a poor Negro. But the captain pulled off his coat and dived into the water and rescued him.

"And what then?" enquired the preacher.

"What den? Why, every breff in my body belongs to him. I wanted to serve him all de rest o' my days. But he wouldn't let me, so I got dis here ferry boat so I could be 'round whenever his boat goes by. An' I do love to point him out!" concluded the Negro with beaming face.

The lesson was obvious. The discouraged preacher took heart and with renewed zeal went on with his task of serving his blessed Master. Devoted and humble witnesses who "love to point Him out" are much needed in these days. They are like the three hundred, vessels "meet for the Master's use."

CHAPTER 8

THE SWORD OF THE LORD

Judges 7:9-22

THE fearful and the careless had all departed when the shades of night began to fall on Gideon and his three hundred. Then the Lord spoke to Gideon, saying, "Arise, get thee down unto the host; for I have delivered it into thine hand." That command should have been enough for Gideon, but the Lord, having full knowledge of the weakness Gideon felt, was prepared to give him further assurance of victory. "But *if* thou fear to go down, go thou with Phurah thy servant down to the host; and thou shalt hear what they say; and afterwards shall thine hands be strengthened."

Gideon accepted that "if." He felt the weakness of his hands and was not ashamed to accept the proffered strengthening. True faith always feels its own weakness, as is illustrated in the man who cried, with tears, "Lord, I *believe!* Help Thou mine *unbelief!*" (Mark 9:24). Therefore, taking with him his trusted servant Phurah, who had helped him destroy the altar of Baal, Gideon crept down under cover of darkness to the camp of the Midianites in the valley.

If there was a moon that night, the sight of that sleeping host must have been impressive, their lines of tents stretching down the valley farther than the eye could see, "their camels without number, as the sands by the sea side for multitude." No doubt there were sentinels about the camp, but if the Midianites had heard anything of the departure of the fearful and careless thousands (and it is likely that they had heard), they were not expecting an attack and their guard was not very alert. It was not difficult, therefore, for Gideon and Phurah to creep into the camp undetected.

1. A Dream and its Interpretation (vv. 13-15)

As they stole along in the darkness, Gideon and Phurah were suddenly arrested by the sound of voices in a tent near by. A man who had just awoke from sleep was relating a dream he had had to a companion. The dream in itself was not very impressive. In his dream he had seen "a cake of barley-bread" come rolling down the hill into the camp and strike one of the tents with such violence that (believe it or not!) it forced down the tent, tearing up the stakes, so that the tent lay alongside and buried its inhabitants! What strange, incoherent things we dream!

But, after all, "do not interpretations belong to God?" (Gen. 40:8). God had caused this man to have such a dream and he caused his fellow to offer an interpretation. Ruefully the other declared, "This is nothing else save the sword of Gideon, the son of Joash, a man of Israel: for into his hand hath God delivered Midian, and all the host." How it must have thrilled Gideon to hear these words! His soul was exalted and he worshiped. To the Midianite the barley cake was "the sword of Gideon" but to Gideon it was "the sword of the Lord *and* of Gideon" (v. 20). Jehovah and he were as one.

Let this object lesson to Gideon be one to us also. First we learn that "this is the victory that overcometh the world, even our faith" (1 John 5:4). It is a blessed thing to see our enemies from faith's viewpoint and to be told that the Lord has delivered them into our hands. Nothing could be more alarming than to see the fearful odds against us, the world, the flesh and the mighty power of Satan. Surely we would faint if this were all the picture, but it is not all. If we are walking in the power of the Spirit of God as risen with Christ, we see Satan and the world and the flesh all under our feet.

Then we learn that even in the camp of the enemy there is a premonition of defeat. Because the great multitudes are on the opposite side, the men of the world seek to persuade themselves that Christianity is false, but down deep in their hearts they know better. Sometimes God is pleased to let us know what is in the hearts of our enemies. How often "what they say" encourages us and strengthens our hands for the conflict as it did Gideon's.

The portrait of Gideon given by the dreamer was not a flattering one. Gideon could not feel elated because of it. He was made to feel that in himself he was nothing. Barley was the food of the poorest, and a cake of barley bread was a fit figure of utter insignificance in contrast with the tent it strikes. In days past Christians were content to be like that "barley cake." Oh, for a return to the simplicity of former days!

Finally, we learn how faith can worship in the full

confidence of victory. Nothing could be more homely
than Gideon as a "barley cake," nothing more dignified
than Gideon as a worshiper. There would be more
abounding praise ascending to God on high if we were
willing to take the place of the cake of barley bread.

2. Trumpets, Lamps and Pitchers (v. 16)

Like his ancestor Abraham, who with three hundred
and eighteen men made a successful night attack on
the army of four victorious kings (Gen. 14:14, 15),
Gideon returned to his three hundred men and prepared immediately for an attack on the Midianites. He
divided the company into three groups and to each
man he gave a trumpet, a lamp and a pitcher.

In 2 Corinthians 4, the Apostle Paul gives us a key
to the understanding of this remarkable Old Testament
picture. "We preach not ourselves, but Christ Jesus
the Lord" (v. 5)—there we have the trumpets. "The
light of the knowledge of the glory of God" shining
"in our hearts" (v. 6) suggests the lamps within the
pitchers. "We have this treasure hid in earthen vessels"
(v. 7)—there are the pitchers. Verses 8-11 suggests
the breaking of the pitchers that the light may shine
forth.

Trumpets speak of the Word of God given in testimony to and by His people. To the Thessalonians Paul
said, "From you sounded out the word of the Lord"
(1 Thess. 1:8). Instructions for the manufacture and
use of the trumpets are given in Numbers 10:1-10.

First, the trumpet was the signal for the gathering
together of the people (v. 3). Gideon had so used it
(Jud. 6:34). He was God's messenger for the gather-

ing again of a people who had been scattered by their own failure. Mary Magdalene was a good gatherer, too. She testified to the disciples of the risen Lord as He instructed her. That same evening found them gathered together with Jesus in the midst (John 20: 11-19).

The trumpet also sounded for the march (vv. 5, 6). No other directions are given for our journey through this desert waste than the word of God.

Then again the trumpet sounded for battle (v. 9). There can be no testimony here for God without conflict for the world is opposed to God. When the trumpet is blown in the face of the foe it is faith's boast in the assurance of God's victory. Jericho's walls fell and the Midianite hosts fled at the sound of the trumpet.

The trumpet also sounded for the solemn feasts of Israel (v. 10). Thus the walk, warfare and worship of God's people is all regulated by the Word of God.

The second factor in the equipment of Gideon's army was the vessels his men carried in their left hands. These vessels held lamps within them. The empty pitchers perhaps had contained the victuals of the people (see v. 8) and though now empty and worthless they were to be used in the service of God for the deliverance of His people. Those vessels were fit symbols of the men who held them, and of the believer as a witness for God in the world. No doubt Paul alludes to this very scene when he writes concerning the "manifestation of the truth" and the display of "the light of the gospel of the glory of Christ." He says, "But' we have this treasure in earthen vessels, that the excellency of the power may be of God and not of us" (2 Cor. 4:7). Clearly he refers to these bodies of ours,

this "mortal flesh" in which the life of Jesus is to be
made manifest.

> "Earthen vessels, marred unsightly,
>   Bearing wealth no thought can know,
> Heavenly treasure gleaming brightly,
>   Christ revealed in saints below."

So long as the vessels that contained the light were
unbroken they were useless; they only hid the light
that was within. It was the breaking of the vessel
that brought into view the bright shining of the light.
This breaking of the vessel is a process we naturally
shrink from and yet it is essential to bearing testimony
to Christ. Look at Stephen, the light beamed forth
from his face when the stones were hurled at him by
his murderers. The light of the glory shining down
into his heart was released from that broken vessel.
The stones of an angry mob may never reach us, there
may be no chance of our being Stephens, but what the
stones did for Stephen the circumstances of life can do
for us. Trials and tribulations, perplexities and perse-
cutions and distresses all serve to break the vessel.
How the beauteous graces of Christ shone out from
the poor smashed earthen vessel in Stephen's case.
"Lord lay not this sin to their charge," he cried, the
echo of the words of the Saviour on the cross, "Father,
forgive them, for they know not what they do."

Of William Hake someone remarked, "Oh, well, he's
cracked." Immediately the reply was given, "The crack
serves well to let the light shine."

The lesson of the smashed earthen vessel is the lesson
of "no confidence in the flesh," an advanced study in
the school of God. Oh, for grace to learn this lesson
in our hearts in the presence of God! There can be

no victory over the foe without it. God only glorifies Himself in instruments which He has broken.

> "Oh, to be but empty, lowly,
> Mean, unnoticed and unknown,
> Yet to God a vessel holy,
> Filled with Christ and Christ alone!
>
> "Naught of earth to cloud the Glory,
> Naught of self the light to dim,
> Telling forth Christ's wondrous story:
> Broken, empty — filled with Him."

The lamps are the third and most important factor in testimony for God. They speak of Christ, He is the light and He is seen when self is hidden. The one purpose of the pitcher was to hold the light.

The illustration has been used of the Statue of Liberty in New York harbor. That lofty structure commands the entrance to the harbor and the attention of every one passing along that busy waterway. Every eye gazes upon it. But when night falls, there blazes from the torch held aloft by the statue's uplifted hand a light. When the light shines the hand that holds it is hidden in the shadow of the light it holds. The light and not the statue is seen and thus it is with the believer. In this world's darkness we are to bear testimony not to ourselves but to Christ.

Are we taking our ease down here, having all we need in this world, finding favor with men who know not God, and experiencing very little of what the apostle enumerates in 2 Corinthians 4:8-11? If so, there is little wonder that the light is dim. How can our God count us worthy to bear a single ray of the light of Christ before the world?

3. Gideon's Strategy (vv. 16-22)

Every member of Gideon's band was a picked man. Every one was fit to be captain of a thousand in the original army of thirty-two thousand men. Every one therefore could be depended on to do the part assigned to him at the proper time and in the proper manner. The strategy of Gideon, no doubt divinely inspired, was to take the enemy completely by surprise and to give the impression that a huge host had surrounded them. The ruse was remarkably successful. A tremendous blast from three hundred ram's horns broke the midnight stillness, three hundred brilliant lights suddenly flared where a moment before there was black darkness, and fom three hundred lusty throats rose the cry, "The sword of the Lord and of Gideon!"

Frightened and confused, the sleeping Midianites scrambled to their feet with but one thought in the mind of each — escape! Every man who blocked the way of another became a victim of his neighbor's sword. Gideon's men, well organized and alert, were complete masters of the situation. In all this there are important lessons for us. Let us notice the *leader* of this band, their *obedience* and their *order*.

Their Leader (vv. 17, 18)

Three companies surrounded the camp of the Midianites, one hundred men in each company, but one captain commanded them all. His word was supreme. "Look on me and as I do, so shall ye do." Thus spoke the leader of the hosts. And this was the answer to the prevailing condition of Israel that had brought on the disaster, for every man had done that which was right in his own eyes. Every eye was to be on Gideon, not even on their companions, and as he did they were to do likewise. One will controlled all their movements, they were to act as one man. Thus there would be unity of action.

Christ is our leader, He is the Captain of our Salvation. There are many assemblies of the saints but He is the Master of Assemblies, the one Shepherd who directs all. We are exhorted to look off unto Jesus, and if we do we are assured of final and complete victory, for He is the "Finisher" of our faith as well as the "Author" (Heb. 12:2).

Their Obedience (vv. 19, 20)

It was not long after midnight, the middle watch having been newly set, when the three companies reached their stations. They were well instructed and they did as they were told. There was no dissension in their ranks, all "three companies blew the trumpets, and brake the pitchers, and held the lamps in their left hands, and the trumpets in their right hands to blow withal: and they cried, The sword of the Lord, and of Gideon." This was their battle cry, their shout of victory. The sword which smote Midian was the sword of Jehovah and none other. Gideon was but the instrument in His hands. What would Gideon's name have been, severed from Jehovah's? What is a cipher without the figure which alone gives it value? Gideon alone was nothing to be accounted of, but Jehovah and Gideon were invincible. In the darkness of that night the hosts of Midian fled, put to flight by that shout following the blare of the trumpets and the flare of the torches. Confusion reigned in the camp of the enemy. Fleeing from death they met it at every turn, for "the Lord set every man's sword against his fellow even throughout all the host."

Obedience paves the path to victory, disobedience always spells defeat. May God teach us to win the victories as Gideon and his men did.

Their Order (vv. 21, 22)

Of the Colossian believers Paul could say, though absent from them, that he rejoiced "beholding their order and the steadfastness of their faith in Christ." The word he used is a military metaphor. It suggests that solid front and orderly array that faith presents to the foe. It was thus the enemy was foiled in Nehemiah's day. The people were set in their appointed places "every one unto his work" (Neh. 4:13-15). There are to be no idle soldiers in the Lord's army. He has gone to heaven, we occupy till He comes again. He has given to "every man his work and commanded the porter to watch" (Mark 13:34).

Every Saturday evening for forty odd years a servant of God stood on a certain street corner handing out gospel papers to the passersby. And then he stopped. Discouraged because he saw so little fruit, he abandoned his post. Some years later he happened on the spot and a young man stood there and gave him a gospel paper. He stopped, addressing the young man he said,

"How is it that you are here tonight?"

"Well, sir, it is like this: an old man occupied this corner for years; I was saved by means of a tract he gave me. Evidently the old man's in heaven now for I've missed him here and so I am seeking to fill his place."

Tears filled the eyes of the older Christian as the young man thus spoke.

"I am the man who gave you that tract," he said, "and by the grace of God I mean to stand in my place till Jesus comes."

Let us learn a lesson from this narrative, that we may "stand fast in one spirit, with one mind striving together for the faith of the gospel; and in nothing terrified by our adversaries; which is to them an evident token of perdition, but to us of salvation and that of God" (Phil. 1:27, 28).

CHAPTER 9

COMPLETE VICTORY

Judges 7:21 - 8:17

*T*HE defeat which Midian suffered at the hands of Gideon and his three hundred was final and complete. Never again did that nation rise to oppose the people of God. Isaiah later used this incident to illustrate the coming deliverance of Israel from their final oppressor. "For Thou hast broken the yoke of his burden, and the staff of his shoulder, the rod of his oppressor, as in the days of Midian . . . And the Lord of hosts shall stir up a scourge for him according to the slaughter of Midian at the rock of Oreb" (Isa. 9:4; 10:26). The battle was with "confused noise and garments rolled in blood," but Gideon's band fought with burning lamps and they had "fuel of fire" or oil in their lamps (Isaiah 9:5).

1. The Flight of the Midianites (vv. 21, 22)

The Midianites fought with carnal weapons but their swords were bathed in their own blood. Gideon's band fought the powers of darkness with Jehovah's sword —lamps and trumpets, symbols of the spiritual weapons of our warfare. Antichrist will be destroyed by the brightness of Christ's coming (II Thess. 2:8) and all

76

his vast armies will be slain in a manner similar to that of the Midianites. Just as Gideon's three hundred were on the hilltop and the enemy below was thrown into confusion and utter rout, so the glorified saints will appear from above to the consternation of the wicked in the day when the trumpet of the Lord shall sound.

"All the host ran and cried and fled," pursued by the Israelites. The route they took in their flight brought them to "Beth-shittah in Zererath, and to the border of Abel-meholah, unto Tabbath" (v. 22). Beth-shittah they found to be indeed answering to its name —"the house of the scourge." The Midianites had chastised the children of Israel; now they in turn felt the sting of the scourge. Zererath means "oppression" and oppression ceased as the rod of the oppressor was broken by the hand of Jehovah (Isa. 9:4), while at Abel-meholah—"mourning of dancing"—the night of pleasure was changed into fear and mourning (Isa. 21:4).

2. The Gathering of the Israelites (vv. 23, 24)

The effect of the victory was to unify the nation. Three hundred men wrought in the energy of faith; all Israel joins in the triumphs of victory. Out of Naphtali and Asher and Manasseh they came to pursue after the Midianites. It did not take a great deal of faith to do that. It is comparatively easy to join in the pursuit of the foe and share the spoils when faith has already won the victory.

Having proved the blessedness of simple dependence upon God, we like Gideon can call upon others to have fellowship with us. Ephraim had not come to

the help of his brother Manasseh, but Gideon sent messengers throughout all mount Ephraim, saying, "Come
down against the Midianites and take before them the
waters unto Beth-barah and Jordan." Ephraim responded immediately and rendered excellent service in
cutting off the enemy's retreat by the lower fords of
Jordan while Gideon pursued them over the upper fords,
crossing the river just south of where it flows from
Lake Galilee.

3. The Slaughter of Oreb and Zeeb (v. 25)

Two of the Midianite princes who tried to escape
through the land of Ephraim were caught. "And they
slew Oreb upon the rock Oreb, and Zeeb they slew at
the winepress of Zeeb, and they pursued Midian, and
brought the heads of Oreb and Zeeb to Gideon on the
other side of Jordan." These Midianites had forced
Israel to take to the rocks for shelter and Gideon, you
remember, had lately hid his corn by the winepress of
Ophrah. Now these Midianites reaped what they had
sown. At the rock and by the winepress they received
the due reward of their deeds; and the places were
named for them to their perpetual infamy.

Both the rock and the winepress speak of the cross
of Christ. Gideon secured his wheat at the winepress
and found acceptance through the offering at the rock.
Where faith proves that "God is for us" the foe finds
His anger burns against him. Oreb, "the raven," and
Zeeb, "the wolf," speak of the powers of darkness with
which we are in conflict. The raven in contrast to the
dove is the unclean bird, at home away from the ark
feeding on corruption (Gen. 8:7). The wolf is the
natural enemy of the sheep, "not sparing the flock"

(Acts 20:29). The power of both is broken at the cross of Christ.

4. The Chiding of Ephraim (ch. 8:1-3)

"A brother offended is harder to be won than a strong city, and contentions are like the bars of a castle" (Prov. 18:19). "He that is slow to anger is better than the mighty, and he that ruleth his own spirit than he that taketh a city" (Prov. 16: 32). Gideon's victory in controlling his own spirit and mollifying the wounded spirit of the men of Ephraim was greater than his victory over the Midianites.

When the men of Ephraim came to him bringing the heads of Oreb and Zeeb, "they did chide with him sharply." "Why hast thou served us thus," they demanded, 'that thou calledst not us when thou wentest to fight with the Midianites?" How easily Gideon might have retorted, "Where were you during all the years that Midian oppressed us?" but he did not do so. With a soft answer he turned away the wrath of these offended brethren. He belittled his own accomplishments and magnified their success in overcoming Oreb and Zeeb. Pointing to the heads of these slain princes, he inquired, "What have I done now in comparison to you? Is not the gleaning of the grapes of Ephraim better than the vintage of Abiezer?" Thus Gideon achieved a remarkable victory.

In all that, Gideon did not justify the chiding of Ephraim. Those men were filled with a sense of their own importance. They considered themselves the leading tribe in Israel. Back in the days of Joshua they had complained of the portion allotted to them. "Why hast thou given me but one lot and one portion to in-

herit seeing I am a great people?" (Joshua 17:14).
When self looms up great before our eyes, there will
be little rejoicing in what God has wrought through
others. The envy that springs from pride is a constant
source of strife between brethren. Conflict with the
world is far less painful and trying than this inward
strife.

Gideon met the situation with an entire setting aside
of self. Having met the God of peace at the altar which
he named Jehovah-shalom ("the Lord send peace"), he
became a peacemaker and qualified for the blessing
pronounced on such by our Lord (Matt. 5:9). By lowly-
mindedness he averted shame and sorrow and division
in Israel.

If Jephthah, in a similar situation, had acted on the
same principle as Gideon, his life's story would not
have been stained with the blood of needless slaughter
(Jud. 12:1-6). Again "the envy of Ephraim" (Isa.
11:13) manifested itself, but Jephthah had no soft answer for their wrath. He returned railing for railing
and further wounded their pride with bitter and sting-
ing accusations. He took up the sword against them
and forty-two thousand Ephraimites fell at that time.
There is little glory in slaying one's brethren. How
much better was the suffering grace of Gideon than
the righteous wrath of Jephthah.

Nothing so appeases contention as a Christlike spirit.
As pride genders contention, so humility and meekness
gender peace. The goal of Christian experience is "to
be likeminded, having the same love, being of one ac-
cord, of one mind" (Phil. 2:2). The means by which
that goal is reached is, "Let this mind be in you, which
was also in Christ Jesus . . ." (v. 5).

A beautiful legend illustrates the excellency of meekness and humility. Long ago there lived a saint of God who went about his daily life diffusing light, as a flower emits perfume, without being aware of it. Two words characterized his life—he *gave* and he *forgave*. Yet these words never fell from his lips; they were only expressed in his smile, in his forbearance and love.

Angels observed him and asked God that the gift of miracles might be given to this man. The desire was granted. So the angels spoke to him and said, "What would you desire?" He said, "That God would give me His grace." When pressed still further to choose the particular power he would have, he replied, "That I may do a great deal of good without ever knowing it."

5. The Baseness of Succoth and Penuel (vv. 4-9)

Self-satisfied, Ephraim returned from the fray, nursing the injured pride salved by Gideon's gentle speech. But for Gideon and the three hundred, the conflict was not over. Leaving the rest of Israel to be satisfied with what spoil they could pick up, they pressed on to complete victory. Coming to Jordan, they passed over the river, "faint, yet pursuing" the foe.

Hungry and weary, worn by a sleepless night, they well deserved a rest. But the same spirit that would not kneel down in comfort to drink, upheld them to press on. They knew Him who "giveth power to the faint, and to them that have no might He increaseth strength" (Isa. 40:29). "Faint and resting," "faint and giving up," would have been a far easier course to follow, but then these words would not have continued down the ages as the proverb descriptive of the Christian race and warfare—"Faint, yet pursuing." Fainting is never a reason for stopping; it is an excellent reason for drawing upon the resources we have in Christ. His fulness, the supply of grace, is always available for the believer.

As Gideon pressed on, "faint, yet pursuing," he came to Succoth and Penuel, two cities of Israel where fresh trials awaited him. Succoth, which means "booths," was where they should have known that "tent dwellers" possessed the land, that faith was greater than sight. Penuel was where Jacob had wrestled with God and proved the power of weakness. Penuel means "the face of God," and certainly those who see God's face fear not that of man. Gideon could reasonably expect help from these people, but when he asked for bread he received a stone. "Give, I pray you, loaves of bread unto my people that follow me; for they be faint, and I am pursuing after Zebah and Zalmunna, kings of Midian."

But the men of Succoth and Penuel were not what they should have been. Snug and secure in their own nests, they renounced all responsibility and refused to supply refreshment to their faint and weary brethren. "Are the hands of Zebah and Zalmunna *now* in thine hand, that we should give bread unto thine army?" And so Gideon and his men were left without the sorely needed refreshment to continue after the Midianites— "faint, yet pursuing."

> "With each countenance turned to the orient side,
> Come on the Three Hundred to Jordan's swift tide;
> Jehovah had called them, and onward they go,
> So weary and 'faint, yet pursuing' the foe.

"O Lord, give us hearts to pursue without fear,
  Though Succoth may slander and Penuel sneer;
For yet a brief space by the power of our God,
  And Satan himself 'neath our feet shall be trod.

"Would'st thou seek any solace, or turn from the fray,
  When the Lord of the battle is leading the way?
'Tis JESUS that calls us, and forward we go,
  Though weary and 'faint, yet pursuing' the foe."

6. The Capture of the Kings (vv. 10-13)

"Make . . . their princes as Zebah and Zalmunna who said, Let us take to ourselves the houses of God in possession. O my God, make them like a wheel, as the stubble before the wind, as the fire burneth a wood, and as the flame setteth the mountains on fire" (Ps. 83:11, 12).

Could a more unequal battle be imagined than that of stubble and the wind, or fire and the wood of the forest? And such is the picture used by the Psalmist as he thinks of the final onslaught of Jehovah's enemies and His triumph over them. But such was not the picture presented to the worldly-minded when Gideon went forth to capture the kings of Midian. Fifteen thousand of the Midianites remained, rallied round the standard of their two kings. They had taken their position on the other side Jordan in Karkor. They thought themselves secure there, as the word puts it, "the host was secure." Karkor means "city of destruction,"—how could there be any security there? And such is the world to all who trust in it. An old saint said, "Do not build your nest in any tree for the whole forest is doomed to destruction." Thinking themselves beyond the danger zone, the world will enjoy a false security in the last days. "For when they shall say,

Peace and safety, then sudden destruction cometh upon them . . . and they shall not escape" (I Thess. 5:3).

Gideon went up "by the way of them that dwell in tents" (v. 11). The pilgrim way is the way of victory over the world. Abraham, Isaac and Jacob dwelt in tents; they were content to have nothing when they possessed all. The path of the Christian is such today. As to title, all is his, faith enjoys its portion, but to sight he has nothing to show. He is on the way to glory but it is the "way of them that dwell in tents," and only faith can see in that pilgrim band the heirs of glory. "You say you are kings and priests with God, and that you are to have glory," is the taunt of unbelief, "but you cannot show us anything for it; when we see you in the glory we will believe." They shall see. By and by the tables will be turned and the taunts and reproaches of the world will bring down judgment upon their own heads. Jude tells us that all the hard speeches which ungodly sinners have spoken will receive their due recompense. Not a single word uttered against the saints that He will not take up in that day as directed against Himself (Jude 15).

Gideon came upon the host unawares. As a thief in the night, finding "the host secure," he fell upon them with his weary men and "discomfited all the host." The morning sun smiled upon a scene of complete victory. A new day has begun for Israel. "Gideon returned from battle before the sun was up."

The names of the kings suggests the power of Satan, for Zebah means "a slaughter made in sacrifice," and many are the victims of Satan's cruel cunning. Zalmunna means "a forbidden shadow"; souls in darkness know not how strong is its grip. Our warfare is with the rulers of this world's darkness, but God will shortly bruise Satan under our feet.

7. The Judgment of False Brethren (vv. 13-17)

There is a striking difference between Gideon's attitude toward the men of Ephraim and his attitude toward those of Succoth and Penuel. The reason is obvious. The Ephraimites, in spite of their pride and jealousy, were true brethren. They rendered yeoman service to Gideon in his struggle against the Midianites. Not so the others. Though the names of their cities were venerable with antiquity and brought to mind some of Jacob's dealings with God, these men were false brethren. Gideon exhibited remarkable patience with his true brethren, but he had none with the false.

Returning in triumph from the battle of Karkor, Gideon taught the men of Succoth a painful but well-deserved lesson—well-deserved because of their base refusal to give a morsel of food to the gallant three hundred, and because, though warned by Gideon, they did not repent of their hardness of heart. The three hundred, so lately despised by the men of Succoth, became Gideon's ministers of justice for their punishment. Catching a young man of Succoth, they enquired of him and got a written list (as the Hebrew indicates) of the elders and princes of Succoth—seventy-seven men in all — together, no doubt, with their places of abode.

When these men were rounded up, they were brought before Gideon, who said, "Behold, Zebah and Zalmunna, with whom ye did upbraid me . . ." The men of Succoth were speechless. By their words they had condemned themselves. Their punishment was sore, but no worse than their crime. Gideon tore their flesh "with the thorns of the wilderness and with briers" (v. 7). These sinners, who were at ease in their Zion while others pursued the enemy through the wilderness, were made to feel in their own flesh the hardships the others had endured. Thus Gideon *"taught* the men of Succoth."

Penuel came next. Its punishment was even more severe, perhaps because its inhabitants had been even more abusive and insolent than those of Succoth. "He beat down the tower of Penuel"—that strong tower in which they had such pride and in which they trusted —"and slew the men of the city." May we learn the lesson that it is better to suffer afflictions with the people of God than judgment in the day of retribution.

CHAPTER 10

SHADOWS

Judges 8:18-35

IF Gideon were a hero of fiction, his story might well end with his return in triumph from the pursuit of the Midianites. But he was "a man subject to like passions as we are," and the Holy Spirit faithfully records his history down to the end. We have seen in Gideon those qualities that mark him out as a Spirit-filled man. In our closing scenes of his life we see shadows that dim the brightness of his character and eventually we find Gideon failing in what was his strongest point. Two characteristics were continued in Gideon in a marked degree — humility and faith. Yet it was in humility that Gideon failed. How often victories find us off our guard. When we face the foe our weakness is only too apparent. There is nothing that we can do but to trust in the might of another. Cast upon the Lord, trusting in Him, we see all our foes defeated. Then, measuring our strength with that of a defeated foe, we are apt to overestimate it and forget that it was God and not ourselves who gained the victory. This we see in Gideon.

1. The Shadow of Flattery (vv. 18-21)

The vanquished kings were not sparing in their praise of Gideon. Gideon had asked them, "What manner of men were they whom ye slew at Tabor?" And they answered, "As thou art, so were they; each one resembled the children of a king." Here was the first bit of flattery and its result. He who had said of himself, "My family is poor," and "I am the least," and was likened to a "cake of barley bread" is now likened to a member of a royal family. We must beware of the flattery of the world and distrust it. The world flatters us to enfeeble us and to divert us from the divine path.

Paul refused the commendation that came from the ranks of the enemy. (See Acts 16:17, 18.) We cannot say that on this occasion Gideon was turned aside from God's path by the speech of the kings, but it did seem to give him an undue sense of his own strength and importance. Gideon entrusted to his son Jether the task of slaying the two kings. Surely this was underrating the strength of the enemy. To Ephraim he had said, "*God* hath delivered into your hands the princes of Midian, Oreb and Zeeb." Here he committed to a youth the destruction of an enemy he despised. Thus Joshua had considered Ai, after the razing of Jericho when the city fell. Joshua measured Ai's strength with Israel's and said, "Make not all the people to labour thither for they are but few." The result was a bitter lesson for Israel, but defeat led to dependence. (See Josh. 8:1.) Joshua evidently learned the lesson, for later on when he made prisoners of five kings, far from underrating their strength in the eyes of the men of Israel, he said, "Fear not, nor be dismayed, be strong and of good courage."

When Jether feared to draw his sword, those kings said to Gideon, "Rise thou, and fall upon us; for as

the man is, so is his strength." Here was a fresh bit
of flattery for Gideon. We do not know how it affected
Gideon but we do know that he had learned differently
in the school of God. The strength in which Gideon
had gone forth to the deliverance of Israel was not the
strength of a man. Had he not been told this by the
angel of Jehovah, upon his confession of Israel's sad
plight and this remembrance of the mighty deeds of
Jehovah, "Go in this thy might"? (ch. 6:13, 14). The
word of the kings has become a proverb to this day
but it is not the language of faith. We look to a Man
in heaven and say, "As that Man is, so is our strength."
Paul could say, "I can do all things," but it was only
"through Christ who strengtheneth me."

2. The Shadow of Self-Glory (vv. 22-27)

Having escaped the snare set by the flattery of the
kings, Gideon was exposed to a new one and more
dangerous. The men of Israel came to Gideon and
said, "Rule thou over us, both thou and thy son, and
thy son's son also: for thou hast delivered us from
the hand of Midian." They put Gideon in the stead
of Jehovah. They desired to exalt him and place the
scepter in his hand and the crown upon his brow.
But Gideon said unto them, "I will not rule over you,
neither shall my son rule over you: the Lord shall rule
over you." Thus Gideon escaped another snare.

Not all the Lord's servants are like-minded. How
many exercise authority over the flock of God. How
prone we are to clericalism, how readily the people
of God foster a Diotrephes (3 John 9) when faith
is weak. The object of true ministry is that Christ
may have the pre-eminence and that all should be

subject to the authority of Him who is Lord of all. Growth in grace is seen in our refusing a place for self. Paul refused to exercise authority. He might have settled matters in Corinth had he gone there, but he refrained from going. "Not for that we have dominion over your faith, but are helpers of your joy; for by faith ye stand" (2 Cor. 1:24).

Gideon refused the crown but he requested the gold. His desire for some memorial of the victory turned him to the path of error. "And Gideon said unto them, I would desire a request of you, that ye would give me every man the earrings of his prey. And they answered, We will willingly give them." Seventeen hundred shekels of gold were collected and many other valuables. With this treasure Gideon made an ephod and put it in his city, in Ophrah.

The oak in Ophrah (6:11), the winepress there, the altar and the rock (6:24, 26)—all had borne testimony to the Lord. No doubt Gideon intended that the ephod should be for God's glory, too, but there was a fly in the ointment—"the thing became a snare to Gideon and to his house." Instead of bringing glory to God, the ephod brought glory to Gideon and displaced the worship of Jehovah in Ophrah. The exact opposite of the broken vessels through which the light shone was this ephod in Ophrah. Only the priests of Jehovah wore the ephod representing the people in the presence of God. Gideon who had declined the crown aspired to the priesthood. Religious power is more subversive than civil power and leads to idolatry.

They were hanging up ephods in Corinth; they gloried in men. "You cannot give me an ephod," said Paul. "Who then is Paul, and who is Apollos?" Others might boast in what they had gotten for themselves; Paul gloried in the One who had gotten him and given all to him. Listen to those smashing blows at any ephod erected to man's praise. "That no flesh should glory in His presence." (1 Cor. 1:29.)

Peter wanted to build tabernacles where Christ was supreme in His glory. No doubt his thought was to perpetuate blessing and to secure for the future the conditions of the mount. But blessing is not maintained by man's efforts. There is no security for the continuance of blessing but the continued presence and power of the Holy Spirit of God.

3. The Shadow of the Tomb (vv. 28-35)

In a very few words we have summed up for us the entire period of forty years following the subjugation of the Midianites. There are four panels in the picture presented in these closing verses, the first one singularly bright, the last clouded with the forebodings of disaster.

God's faithfulness (vv. 28, 29). The victory was complete and the blessing that followed covered a long period of continued peace and prosperity. "Thus was Midian subdued before the children of Israel, so that they lifted up their heads no more. And the land was in quietness forty years in the days of Gideon.

Victory over all foes, peace and quietness are blessings to be desired by the people of God. We read of such a season of blessing in Acts 9:31: "Then had the churches rest throughout all Judaea and Galilee and Samaria, and were edified; and walking in the fear of the Lord, and in the comfort of the Holy Ghost, were multiplied." Supplications, prayers and intercessions are to be made in order that "we may lead a quiet and peaceable life in all godliness and honesty."

Following the victory Gideon returned to his own home. "And Jerubbaal the son of Joash went and dwelt in his own house." Notice that his new name is used here, the name he won for himself by contending with Baal. The quiet of his own home and the conflict in his father's are thus brought into vivid contrast. The disturber of the false peace brought true peace.

Gideon's failure (vv. 30, 31). Refusing the crown Gideon accepted the priesthood. Retiring into obscurity he maintained a household and a harem like that of a prince. All this was contrary to the will of God. He had said concerning the ruler of His people, "Neither shall he multiply wives to himself, that his heart turn not away" (Deut. 17:17).

And then, furthermore, Gideon failed in his alliance with a Canaanitish woman (ch. 9:4, 28); he had a concubine in Shechem. And the fruit of this union revealed a spirit quite different from that which marked Gideon when he was in touch with God. He called his son Abimelech, the name by which the Canaanitish lords were designated. Abimelech means "my father is king." That was what Gideon was not, what he refused to be. The name also suggests a "king's father," that is, the founder of a dynasty. It may be that such was the ambitious hope of the mother and Gideon yielded to her desires. At any rate here were sown the seeds of a bitter harvest. The entire house of Gideon, Jothan excepted, was exterminated by this son of a Canaanitish concubine, who set himself up to be king over Israel.

Gideon's funeral (v. 32). That funeral in Ophrah of the Abiezrites must have been impressive. Perhaps the altar was still standing there, and the oak near the winepress where the angel of the Lord first met him. The ephod also was there that marked the beginning of Gideon's decision. They laid him in the sepulcher of Joash his father, and with him into that tomb went the rest Israel had enjoyed during his life.

Israel's folly (vv. 33-35). As soon as Gideon was off the scene "the children of Israel turned again, and went a whoring after Baalim, and made Baalberith their god." God had spoken peace to His people and to His saints, but they had turned again to folly. (See Ps. 85:8.) Back into the bondage out of which they had been delivered they went. "And the children of Israel remembered not the Lord their God who had delivered them out of the hand of all their enemies on every side; neither showed they kindness to the house of Jerubbaal, namely Gideon, according to all the goodness which he had shewed unto Israel." Sad evidence of the waywardness and deceitfulness of the human heart.

And so, at the close of our story, we leave Israel where we found them at the beginning, forgetting the mercies of the Lord and serving the gods of the heathen; and thus, also, a helpless prey to their enemies. Would God now cast off His people? No. Once more, when they had learned the bitterness of their own ways, He would send them a deliverer. "If we believe not, yet he abideth faithful: he cannot deny himself" (2 Tim. 2:14).

Printed in the United States of America